*Weekend Walks*

# DARTMOOR
# AND EXMOOR

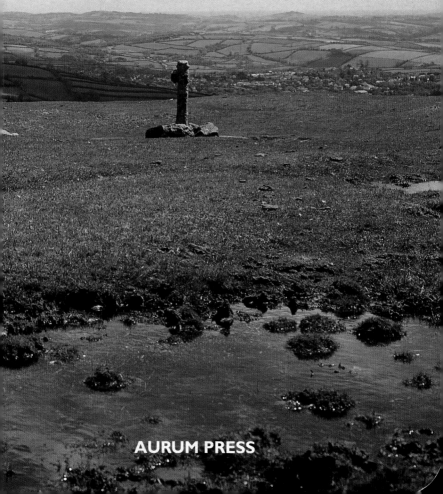

## *Weekend Walks*

# DARTMOOR
# AND EXMOOR

## Anthony Burton

### *Photographs by Mike Williams*

**AURUM PRESS**

First published in Great Britain 2000
by Aurum Press Ltd
25 Bedford Avenue, London WC1B 3AT

Maps reproduced from Ordnance Survey 1:25 000 Pathfinder, Outdoor Leisure
and Explorer map series with the permission of The Controller of Her Majesty's
Stationery Office © Crown copyright: Licence No: 43453U

A catalogue record for this book is available from the British Library.

ISBN  1 85410 676 7

Designed by Robert Updegraff
Printed and bound in Italy
by Printers Srl, Trento

**Title Page** Spurrell's Cross, high on Dartmoor above South Brent.
**Cover** The East Lyn Valley above Watersmeet.

# Contents

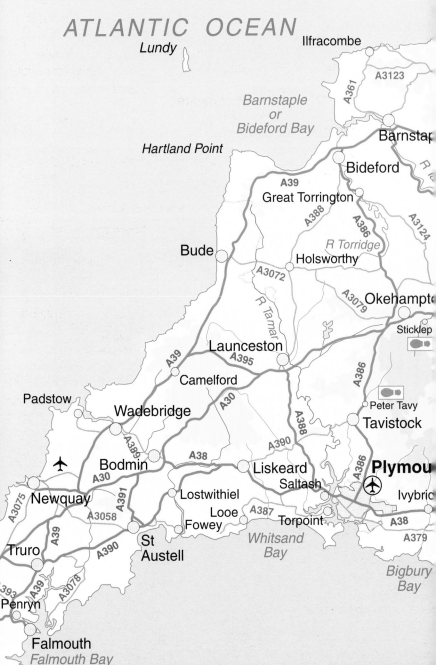

ATLANTIC OCEAN

Lundy

Ilfracombe

A3123

A361

*Barnstaple
or
Bideford Bay*

Barnsta

*Hartland Point*

Bideford

A39

Great Torrington

A388

A386

A3124

*R Torridge*

Bude

A3072

Holsworthy

R l

*R Tamar*

A3079

Okehampto

A395

Launceston

A39

Sticklep

Camelford

A30

Wadebridge

Padstow

A389

A386

Peter Tavy

A388

Tavistock

Bodmin

A38

A390

Liskeard

A386

**Plymou**

A30

A391

Saltash

Newquay

A3058

Lostwithiel

A387

A386

A3075

Looe

Torpoint

Ivybric

St
Austell

Fowey

*Whitsand
Bay*

A38

A379

Truro

A39

A390

*Bigbury
Bay*

A3078

A393

Penryn

Falmouth

*Falmouth Bay*

A tall stone, erected in the Bronze Age, stands in solitary magnificence on a lonely stretch of Dartmoor near Peter Tavy.

# Introduction

The seven walking centres – four on Dartmoor, three on Exmoor – have been selected because excellent walking is available in the countryside around them, and also because they are attractive places in their own right, with reasonable facilities and somewhere to get a meal and slake the thirst at the end of the day. Two walks are described for each centre, starting wherever possible from the town or village itself or from very close by. Most visitors these days arrive by car, and the hope is that the vehicle will not be needed again until it is time to go home at the end of an enjoyable weekend's walking. The walks themselves are all between ten and fifteen miles long and should provide a good, but not overly demanding day's outing.

Inexperienced walkers sometimes have doubts about how long a particular walk might take. A useful guide is Nasmith's rule which suggests a walking rate of 2.5 miles an hour (4km per hour) on the flat, with 4 minutes added for every 100 ft (30 m) climbed. So, for example, on Walk 1 from Lynmouth the total distance is 12.5 miles (20 km) which would suggest 5 hours, but it is very far from flat. The climb up from the start to the top of Old Barrow Hill takes the walker 1130 ft (345 m) above sea level, so that adds another three quarters of an hour right away, and there is a second climb out of the Doone valley up over Malmsmead Hill, so that a realistic walking time would be six hours. That is *walking time* and takes no account of stops along the way, lunch, or anything else. In other words, it is reasonable to think of this as a day's walk. It should be stressed, however, that this is an average. Some walkers will be slower, will stop regularly to admire the view or watch the wildlife; others will put their heads down and keep going all day at a brisk pace.

As the author who devised and walked all these routes, all I can say is that I personally enjoyed all of them immensely and found each of them to be a reasonable and comfortable day's exercise. I hope, by the end, the reader and walker will share my enthusiasm and get as much pleasure as I did from these fourteen walks through some of the best scenery that Dartmoor and Exmoor have to offer.

# DARTMOOR

The 365 square miles (94,535 hectares) of upland not only represents one of the largest areas of wild, open country in England, but also, rising as it does to over 2000 ft (610 m), at the 619-metre summit of High Willhays, contains the highest point in southern England.

Ultimately its character derives from its geological history. An almost inconceivable 400 million years ago, the whole area was under the sea, on the bed of which various sediments were compressed to form layers of shale, slate and sandstone. The first land masses to poke above the surface were the solidified ashes and lavas from underwater volcanoes. Then, some 290 million years ago, great upheavals in the earth's crust thrust up a huge mound of granite, bursting through the earlier sedimental rocks, and carrying them up with it. For another hundred million years, the granite was gradually eroded and then another great change submerged the whole region once again. Chalk was deposited above the granite, and when the sea again retreated it left a high plateau, the basis for modern Dartmoor.

Rivers cut deep down through the chalk which was gradually washed away. The granite hills were attacked by the cold, splitting the rock into the typical horizontal and vertical 'joints' which we see in the tors today, and fragments broke away to form the 'clitter' the shattered rocks that litter the summit slopes. For a time, forest covered much of the area, but as that was cleared by fire and by early settlers, so the peat moorland formed with its typical covering of heather, grass, rush and moss. This early clearing proved disastrous for the would-be farmers, for without protection, erosion soon wore away the poor soil, and whole areas were soon covered in bracken. But the farmers' loss was our gain, for it created the great open space that is such a delight to the walker.

Man first came to the moor in the New Stone Age, around 4000 BC, but left few traces. The most spectacular survivor is the burial chamber known as Spinsters' Rock, which is visited on

Sticklepath Walk 2. The introduction of metal working, first copper then bronze, brought new settlers to the area. The marks of the Bronze Age people who arrived around 1750 BC are everywhere on the moor, perhaps most famously seen in the mysterious stone rows, standing stones and circles. They must once have had some deep religious and ritual significance, but what it was can now never be fully known, though that has not stopped the steady flow of theories, from the tentative and scholarly to the wholly fantastical. Burial chambers in the form of round barrows became prominent features in the landscape, often set on hilltops or ridges, so that they became very obvious eruptions on the skyline. Some of the best examples are passed on Walk 2 from Widecombe-in-the-Moor. That same walk passes the most spectacular of the Bronze Age settlements, Grimspound. Within a high walled enclosure, there are many stone hut circles. These people built their huts with low walls and paved floors, with a central pole supporting a conical roof, presumably covered with turf, bracken and heather.

Iron implements reached the area around 500 BC, and about that time people began the drift away from the high moor. The Iron Age tribes are associated with hill forts, usually situated above the deep valleys at the edge of the moor, such as White Tor Fort on Walk 1 from Peter Tavy. The central moor then remained largely untouched and unpopulated until Saxon times, when settlements were again established in more sheltered spots round the edge of the moor, with occasional fields being established as terraces up the slopes. A rare example of a medieval village some way out on the moor can be seen at Houndtor, where the remains of houses built and lived in between c.1250 and 1350 survive (Walk 1, Widecombe) But if the poor land proved unproductive for crops, it was quite suitable for grazing sheep and cattle, as it still is today.

There was another attraction which drew men to the moor, the presence of tin ore. At first the tin came from alluvial deposits at or near the surface. First the heavy ore was separated from the lighter gravel by washing, then it was crushed under water-powered stamps and finally smelted in small furnaces, where the temperature was raised by the use of water-powered bellows. All this activity resulted in huge disturbances to the ground, as the miners hunted for new sources and followed the veins, and there are spectacular examples of the work of the old tin streamers on the walks from Buckfastleigh. On the western edge of the moor, copper was also found, but here its extraction involved deep mining. As mines were sunk ever deeper, so problems of flooding increased, and the solution was found in the shape of giant steam engines to pump the pits clear. Wheal Betsy on Peter Tavy Walk 1 is a splendid example of a nineteenth-century engine house. Other industries thrived on the moor, notably quarrying, for Dartmoor granite is a wonderfully durable building stone. The extensive Merrivale quarries met on Peter Tavy Walk 1 are prime examples and the Haytor Granite Tramway is a splendid indication of just what needed to be done to get the stone blocks down from the heights of the moor (Widecombe Walk 1). Other industries also thrived - china clay, and woollen cloth manufacture based on the flocks of sheep that roamed the upland. Dartmoor was very far from being the empty place it can seem today.

In the twentieth century, the old industries decayed and died, and even farming has gone into decline. But Dartmoor has found a new role, admired and visited as an area of wild, natural beauty. In 1951, the region became a National Park with around half the area designated as common land where people can roam freely. The walks in this book have been devised to provide examples of as many aspects of Dartmoor scenery as possible. Some head far out into the common land of the moor, others take in the often very dramatic deep river gorges. At some stage almost every walk includes a feature that is typical of the fringes, a sunken lane, worn deep into the land by centuries of use. The high banks, often topped by hedge or wall, cut out the wide vistas, but more than compensate by sporting a splendidly rich variety of plant life, which in turn provides feasts for birds and insects. In an age when hedgerows are disappearing, the lanes are doubly welcome. It is impossible in such a short introduction to do more than indicate the rich variety of wildlife to be met along the different walks, but personal  memories include a rare sighting of a buzzard, dropping literally like a bolt from the blue, to snatch up a fledgling in mid air, an aloof fox marching unconcernedly down a track in front of me, cheeky little stonechats that seem unmoved by the approaching walker, while the liquid tones of the skylark have provided a welcome accompaniment to many of the walks over high ground. And there are those ubiquitous Dartmoor residents, the wild ponies roaming out among the tors.

Walking on Dartmoor, especially on the open moor, is a splendid experience, but is not without its problems. The terrain is rough. The uplands are stony in parts, boggy in others. Wooded river valleys retain moisture and paths, especially bridleways, are likely to be muddy – and doubly so in wet weather. So, good waterproof walking boots are essential. Real difficulties can arise on the open moorland sections. Because of its height, Dartmoor can be a dangerously inhospitable area in bad weather. Clouds can come right down over the tops, experienced by the walker as a miserable, wet mist, obliterating all the surrounding landscape. This happens in all hill country, but has a special significance on Dartmoor.

Looking at the Ordnance Survey maps for the region, there are the familiar and reassuring dotted green lines indicating footpaths and bridleways, but although these are official rights of way they may not be widely used and so are not recognisable as footpaths on the ground. The reason is simple – open access. Walkers are free to roam, and they do, and as a result a hundred different walkers can choose a hundred different ways to get to the top of a particular hill or reach a tor. A deliberate decision has been taken by the Park authorities not to put signposts on the moor, in order to preserve its wild character, and not even the long-distance Two Moors Way is waymarked. This is not a problem in good visibility, but when everything is lost in the grey dampness, then the walker is entirely reliant on map and compass. The safest approach is to check the local weather forecast and if clouds are already low or likely to come down, then it is best to opt for one of the valley walks. Certainly anyone who has any doubts about their ability to use map and compass correctly should keep well clear of high ground when bad weather threatens. Every effort has been made to make direction finding as easy as possible in this book, but an instruction to aim for a tor on the horizon is no use when all you can see are your own boots.

Weather is always a factor on Dartmoor walks. A strong wind in the valley can be gale force on top, and a cold day will be that much colder. There can be snow that piles into drifts in winter even when the valleys below are quite clear. Even the sunniest of days brings its hazards. It is possible to walk all day with almost no shade, and the sun's rays are at their strongest in the clear air. Equally there are a number of walks where there is nowhere serving anything at all in the way of refreshment, so it is important to remember to take food and far, more importantly, plenty to drink. Finally, the area has a problem all its own – the army firing ranges. In general, there is no firing at weekends nor in the busiest holiday periods. Even so it is always necessary to check – the information on how to do so is given at the end of the book. If you do arrive at a range and the red flags are flying, then you must keep away. At other times, it is perfectly safe though you must never touch anything that looks remotely like ammunition.

Describing problems always tends to make walks seem fraught with perils. They are not. This is one of Britain's great walking areas, and can offer a sense of solitude and grandeur that brings visitors back year after year. The advice is offered to make sure that walks are as safe and enjoyable as they can be.

# EXMOOR

Because the two National Parks of South West England both have the name 'moor' in their names, it is easy to think that walking in one will be much like walking in the other. In fact, the experience is very different, not least because Exmoor includes over 30 miles (50km) of the South West Coast Path along its northern border, and some of the most attractive and dramatic sections have been incorporated into the walks. The scenic differences, as always, have their origin in the aeons of geological time.

Like Dartmoor, Exmoor spent millions of years under the sea, where deposits built up that in time became slates and shales, limestone and, most importantly for the future of the land, sandstone. The same violent upheavals that thrust Dartmoor above the waves lifted Exmoor, but it was spared the second great change that thrust the granite to the surface. Soft sandstone does not weather like hard granite, so what we have today is an interesting, mixed region with a character all its own. It can be thought of as a giant wedge, highest in the north where the cliffs rise over 1000 ft (305m) above the sea. But unlike the cliffs of the south coast or even those further to the west, these rise sheer for just a short way, then slope away at a very steep angle to the top. Behind the cliffs, the land slips more gradually away to the south, until a point is reached where the sandstone has been broken down to form the startlingly rich, red soils of the Somerset plain. The rivers that drain the high moor have cut deep into the land creating the characteristic combes. On their way to the sea, the fast-flowing rivers have carved dramatic, deep gorges, none more so than that of the East Lyn, visited on Walk 1 from Lynmouth. Unlike Dartmoor, where the tors regularly rise on the skyline, Exmoor can seem almost featureless, rising gently and smoothly. That does not make

The tree-shaded stone pathway beside the River Barle that leads towards Tarr Steps on the first Winsford walk.

it dull – far from it. It can seem every bit as lonely and wild as Dartmoor, when all one can see is an expanse of heather stretching off to the horizon and the only company is the mournful call of the curlew. And anyone who takes the walk up Dunkery Beacon from Winsford will find an unforgettable viewpoint. Much of the charm of Exmoor lies in contrasts – little lanes wind their way through gently undulating farmland, suddenly broken into by a lush, tree-filled combe or ending at a high moor with a distant view of the sea.

Man has lived on Exmoor since the Stone Age, though early remains are few. The most significant sites met with on the walks are from the Iron Age, and from the Roman conquest that brought this phase of history to a close. Hill forts rise high above the Barle valley visited on Winsford Walk 1, while the Romans built their own fortresses and signal posts along the coast to warn against invasion. They can be seen on Old Barrow Hill and Martinhoe on the two Lynmouth walks. But centuries of settlement have left their own marks on the land.

The old farms of the uplands were built to withstand the worst the weather could do, with thick, rough stone walls and immense external chimneys, with added protection being given by high hedges and copses. This may be a tough landscape, but the houses seem snuggly settled down in their sheltering hollows. The remains of industrial life are not immediately obvious, but Exmoor did have its importance. Iron ore mining was carried out to a considerable extent in the Brendon Hills, and the fast flowing rivers were a suitable source of power, driving the machinery of woollen mills in the Heddon valley (Lynmouth Walk 2) and for a variety of other processes, notably grinding corn, while on the East Lyn hydroelectric power was in use as early as 1890.

Walking on Exmoor brings great variety. Many of the coastal paths are distinctly vertiginous, and high enough for one to spend more time looking down on seabirds rather than looking up at them. Inland, there is an abrupt transition as farmland of neat, tidy fields gives way to heather moorland, where only a few minutes walking can give the sense of being quite alone in a vast landscape.

Of the wildlife to be seen, the stocky Exmoor ponies are very much a feature of the moor, but by far the most famous inhabitants, the red deer, are more elusive. Few subjects raise more passionate feelings than stag hunting. Opponents should perhaps be aware that many of the local pubs and inns are full of trophies and locals are strong supporters of the hunt. It is possible to walk all day without a sight of a deer, which might be disappointing. In the rutting season, however, which begins in late September, a stag is just about the last thing you want to encounter. These normally reticent beasts become very aggressive and the air rings with their 'belling', a distinctive and alarming noise, half way between a bellow and a roar.

Once again, it is necessary to keep a weather eye open, for if the clouds come down they will cover the tops. Here, however, the National Park contains less open access land, footpaths are generally signposted, and because the heather and bilberry which cover much of the moor make for difficult walking, paths once established tend to be generally followed. Nowhere on the moorland sections is very far from roads and habitation. Here too, the walks have been chosen to reflect the diversity of the region, and all that remains is to wish the reader good walking and many enjoyable weekends on Dartmoor and Exmoor.

# Widecombe-in-the-Moor

A village which to many epitomises Dartmoor, it has a good deal more to offer than just being famous for the song 'Widecombe Fair' – though the fair is still held annually. At its heart is the green with its old inn, sixteenth-century Church House and, dominating everything, the fourteenth-century church itself, with a resplendent, pinnacled tower. In a famous accident of 1638 lightning hit the tower and a pinnacle fell through the roof while a ball of fire hurtled down the nave.

## WALK 1 — Hound Tor and Haytor

11 miles (18 km)  See map on pages 22 and 23

An exhilarating walk that incorporates visits to a deserted medieval village and a unique railway.

There is a quiet start to the walk along the Natsworthy road past the Old Inn **1**. A little stream appears on the right, crosses under the road and then goes off about its own affairs. Meanwhile the view gets ever grander, with a succession of shattered tors, including the oddly named Honeybag Tor. This is a beautiful valley where the lush green of fields contrasts with the more sombre shades of the moorland rising to either side. There are more contrasts up ahead. To the left of the road, a fine array of ornamental trees marks the grounds of Wooder Manor, while to the right is mature woodland with massive boulders lurking between the trees, some of which have been rolled off to the edge to build the boundary wall. Once across the small river, the road begins a steady climb towards the head of the valley marked by farms sitting amid an intricate patchwork of small fields. One farmhouse appears beside the road, with little upper storey windows peering out through a mass of thatch, like eyes peeping through an overgrown fringe. Then the road dips down to the river, but only for a temporary respite for it soon begins to climb again. At the top of this steep little climb, where the road turns sharp left **2**, carry straight on along the footpath that heads up the field, shaded by fine old beech trees. It is worth pausing to look back on Widecombe now far below in the valley.

At the end of the path rejoin the road that takes you first to Lower Natsworthy with its handsome farm and cottages then on to an impressive stand of beech that marks the arrival of Higher Natsworthy. Where woodland ends on the right **3** turn right through the gate onto a broad green track. Once clear of the wood, this high level walk brings a great array of tors into view, the most dramatic of which is the next objective, Hound Tor. Cross straight over the road to continue on the bridlepath. Keep to the fence on the left across two fields and where the fence ends continue straight on passing a solitary gorse bush to head for the gate in the wall **4**.

Turn right onto the road, which brings you to a junction where there is an attractive thatched house with a thatch-covered gateway **5**. Refreshments are available nearby from a place with a groaningly punny name – The Hound of the Basket Meals. From here you head straight across the grass to the rocks of Hound Tor, one of the most spectacular rock formations on Dartmoor. From here one looks straight across to the other major tor to be visited on this walk, Haytor Rocks, which seem to be quite near but we shall be taking a far from direct line. The next immediate objective lies in the hollow beneath the prominent Greator Rocks, the deserted medieval village of Houndtor **A**.

Take the obvious path down through the gorse and the pattern of low stone walls soon becomes clear. You can pick out the remains of eleven stone buildings, which include the  walls of three

The tall tower of Widecombe church, seen from the south against an impressive background of moorland.

A set of 'points' on the unique Haytor granite tramway.

houses, still standing three or four courses high. This is all that remains of a settlement abandoned around 1350. The people here grew oats and rye, had kilns for drying grain and kept animals that seemed to have thrived, so the reasons for leaving the site have never been understood..

From the old village take the obvious sandy path between the rocks, signposted as a bridlepath to Leighon and Haytor Down. It leads downhill along the edge of the woodland and then drops steeply to a clapper bridge over the stream. A pleasant path then wanders up through the wood, turning off to the right to thread a line between trees and boulders, before swinging back to the left to leave the wood. Once clear of the wood, turn left to follow the path beside the trees, with the bracken-covered hill rising up on the right. Where the woodland ends the path continues to take a line beside the stone wall that marks the boundary between farmland and rough moor. There is a brief excursion down a lane, where an enclosure has taken a bite out of the moor on the right. This leads downhill to the cluster of buildings that make up the hamlet of Leighon **6**. Here, where the track divides, carry on uphill on the bridlepath signposted to Upper Terrace Drive. The path climbs up past a small quarry and the scenery changes once again. Over to the left, the tower of Manaton church can be seen, and there are views back to Hound Tor. Eventually the path levels out on gorse-speckled moorland to reach a road **7** where you turn right.

This is a high level road with grassy edges that make for comfortable walking, and looks over wooded hills to the Bovey valley. A fine spread of woodland joins the route briefly on the left. This is Yarner Wood, a national nature reserve. Then, topping a rise, the great granite bulk of Haytor Rocks comes into sight, and the view opens out all the way to the coast. Just before reaching the houses of Haytor Vale, look out for a tall stone on the right, with an unusual track of parallel strips of granite alongside it **8**. This is the remarkable Haytor Granite Tramway, built around 1820 by George Templer – hence the name of the local walk, Templer Way – to link the Haytor stone quarries with the Stover Canal at Teigngrace. Iron was expensive and difficult to transport up onto the moor, but the one thing that was available in quantity was granite. So the line was built with stone 'rails' each being 8ft (2.4m) long and cut to an L-shaped cross section to take the wheels of horsedrawn waggons. It was heavy work and teams of 18 horses headed trains of 12 waggons loaded with stone. In places the blocks have disappeared, but the old line remains clear as a grassy track, heading towards the prominent spoil heaps of the quarry.

As the Haytor Rocks again come into view, the rails split at stone 'points' **9**. You can see a hole bored in the stone, where a metal plate was fixed which could be swivelled to turn waggons onto either route. Take the line to the left heading past the old quarries **B**. Stone from here was used for the British Museum and the old London Bridge, now residing in Arizona. Continue on past the quarries to Haytor Rocks **C**. There is an easy scramble to the top, though rock climbers have devised more complex and demanding routes. From the rocks, turn right following a route parallel to the road, heading for the next rocky summit, Saddle Tor. This is all good open country, and once you reach the second tor, head down to the road towards a car park where the walls mark the start of farmland **10**. These walls provide convenient perches for garrulous stonechats.

Where the moorland route is blocked by a wall, continue along the path at the edge of the road to the T-junction **11** where there is another small car park. Carry straight on forward up the broad, grassy track to the rocky summit of Pil Tor and then turn right along the summit ridge to the piled up rocks of Top Tor. From here there is no particular path down, but you will be joining the road down to Widecombe. The first landmark to aim for is the prominent patch of pine **D**. Carry on to the right of the conifers and continue downhill until the way ahead is blocked by walls. Join the road and continue down, back to Widecombe.

Looking across from the imposing granite summit of Hound Tor to Haytor rocks on the skyline.

**WALK 2**

## Grimspound and Hamel Down

11 miles (18 km)  See map on pages 28 and 29

The walk begins as with Walk 1 by taking the Natsworthy road past the Old Inn, but this time goes no further than the playing fields. Here you turn left up the rough road signposted Grimspound via Hamel Down **1**. There is a steep climb, after which the road gives way to a track, worn down in places to the flat slabs of the bedrock. Eventually a gate leads out onto the open moor **2**. Continue on over grassland, following the line of the wall that separates the gorse-covered hill from the fields. This is a long steady climb and looking back you can see the road winding up from Widecombe to the prominent, hunched rock summit of Haytor. As the track levels out to a short ridge, there are extended views down both flanks. As the wall ends on the right, the route goes straight on, heading for the top of Hamel Down. Stonechats chatter, larks sing and rather fearsome-looking long horned cattle regard the walker with uninterested gaze before returning to the more serious task of grazing. Although this is quite a long climb, it is such a wonderful situation with such immense vistas to enjoy that it all passes quite painlessly. Eventually a stone **A** marks the summit of Hameldown Beacon over 1600 ft (500 m) above sea level and 800 ft (260 m) above the start of the walk. The effort is rewarded by a complete panoramic view.

The way ahead now appears as a pale streak of a path through the dark heather towards two low mounds on the skyline. The first mound appears to the left of the path **B** somewhat enigmatically known as 'Two Barrows' though only one is now evident. This is a circular mound with a sunken centre, one of a group of burial sites dating back to the Bronze Age. There is now great walking along the high ridge, with another similar round barrow beside the path and a much larger one, known appropriately as 'Broad Barrow' up ahead. The path passes to the left of the big barrow, also passing the remains of an old cross before heading off towards the cairn that marks the end of the ridge and the summit of Hameldown Tor. From here one looks across a little valley to tall Hookney Tor and beyond to a procession of hills rolling away to a distant horizon.

The way now continues on the obvious path, heading increasingly steeply downhill. Soon the great round enclosure of Grimspound **C** comes into view in the valley. The circular wall is about 10 ft (3 m) wide and is believed originally to have been up to 7 ft (2 m) high. There is an obvious entrance facing Hamel Down. Once inside, you can see the remains of the circular huts with low stone walls, built in the Bronze Age, and presumably home to the people who in death were buried in the barrows that mark the skyline. It is one of the most important prehistoric sites on Dartmoor.

A flagstone path leads away from the site to the road **3** where you turn right. To the left of the road is an area of greatly disturbed ground, all gulleys and mounds. As the name Headland Warren suggests, this was an area where rabbits were bred, both for meat and fur, but it is all jumbled up with the old tin mine workings. Just past the end of the deep gulley **4** turn sharp left to take the path running through the heather towards the farm. This is a genuine free range farm with sheep, goats, geese and scampering black-spotted pigs. Leave the farmhouse to your left and carry on along the bridleway signposted to Warren House Inn. This sandy path now wanders past another area of rifts and spoil heaps to top a ridge and look down on a ravaged valley, hacked and cut by the miners. Up ahead on the far side is the whitewashed Warren Inn, but our route turns off before reaching it – though the very thirsty can always add an extra mile and a stiff climb to the walk.

Reaching the valley floor a broad green track leads on to a crossing of paths **5** in the middle of an extensive mining area. Turn left onto the path heading towards the woods. This is pleasant, easy walking with marshy ground to the side and a flat heather-covered valley floor closed in by hills. At the edge of the wood where the path divides **6** take the track to the right signposted to Soussons which passes the remains of old mine buildings. Here you turn left onto a typical forest road through the conifers. Where this broad track turns sharply to the left, carry straight on up the much rougher bridleway. Like so many woodland paths this can get quite boggy and muddy in places, but you may be lucky enough, as the author was, to catch a glimpse of a barn owl, a white spectre gliding noiselessly between the trees. The path arrives at a wide forest track and a clearing where you carry straight on to a gate which takes you out of the wood. Continue in the same direction, following the woodland edge, and continue beyond the gate to the path signposted to the road near Grendon. This is scenery with a bit of everything – fields, woods, marshes, hills and on the hillside you can see the long ridges of medieval field boundaries following the contours.

At the road **7** turn right. Just beyond the cattle grid, as the road swings to the right to follow the edge of the wood **8,** carry straight on along the wide track. Stay on this track for a short way across heather moorland, pass an old boundary stone on the left, then where paths cross by a signpost **9,** turn left onto the sandy track across the common. Again there is a change in the landscape, to green, undulating grassland with paler, reedy areas of boggy ground. An avenue of trees can be seen up ahead. The farm track heads straight for them, but this is deceptive. About 650 ft (200 m) before reaching them, look out for a gate on the right and a path which leads across the field to a shallow 'V' in the trees at the point where they meet the road **10**. Turn left onto this most attractive and quiet country lane, with views of hills and tors and a good deal of interest closer at hand. At the road junction where you continue straight on towards Lower Cator, there is a wall built of quarried blocks, instead of the more familiar natural boulders, many of them showing the marks of drilling. Gorse-topped walls now line the route as it heads towards the gently rounded hill of Corndon Down. The road skirting the hill has a grassy margin, which makes for comfortable walking. Continue straight on at the first road junction as the road begins to head downhill, passing an old quarry.

At the next road junction **11** turn left and immediately left again to head down to the bridge across the river, after which the road climbs and twists up the hill on the far side. Where the road levels out turn left onto the sandy track heading up onto the moor **12.** Once through the gate turn right onto the path running through the gorse, keeping the rocky outcrop on the top of the hill to your left. The path comes out by a stone wall which is followed round, eventually turning downhill towards the road. Cross straight over the road by the wall opposite, and now there is no very obvious track to follow. You need to turn at an angle half-right away from the road. You are aiming eventually to join the road coming in on the right. The only obvious landmark is a rock outcrop. Think of this as being at 12 o'clock and head for 10 o'clock. This is easy walking over turf cropped short by ponies and eventually you will reach the road somewhere near the point where the open moor gives way to fields. Turn left to continue up the road, and when you top the rise you will get a now familiar view of the tors above Widecombe with the distinctive shape of Haytor in the distance. There is a steep drop to a T-junction **13** where you turn left to return to the village.

The footpath from Hamel Down seen from the entrance to the Bronze Age settlement of Grimspound.

# Sticklepath

This is an ideal centre for exploring northern Dartmoor, for it stands right on the margin between farmland and moor, dominated by the shapely, rounded bulk of Cosdon Hill. The River Taw was the making of the village, providing power for serge mills and corn mills. It also had a former importance as a stopping place on the A30, but with the construction of the A30T passing a mile to the north, a blessed peace has descended on Sticklepath. There is one fascinating reminder of the industrial past, Finch's Foundry, now open to the public and in the care of the National Trust. A long leat from the river brings water to three wheels that provide the power for the establishment set up by William Finch in 1834 to make agricultural implements. One wheel drives a fan to provide the blast for the hearth where the metal is heated, a second powers immense tilt hammers under which it is then shaped and the third turns a grindstone. It is well worth a visit and also marks the starting point for the first walk. This walk passes through the Okehampton firing range.

## WALK 1   Belstone and Tor Steeperton

10.5 miles (17 km)  See map on page 34

This is very much an open moorland walk, where there is no shelter for most of the way and as it reaches heights of well over 1500 ft (450 m) should not be attempted in bad days of low cloud. On a good day, however, this is a superb introduction to the lonely landscape of the wild moor.

The walk begins at Finch's Foundry in the main street of Sticklepath **1**. Go through the arch by the entrance and through to the car park. Carry on past an attractive little summer house and a graveyard to a gate on the left with a signpost to 'Museums Walk via a footbridge'. The path beyond the gate leads through a wood of mainly silver birch to the River Taw and a footbridge **2** which you cross. Once over this turbulent stream turn right on the riverside path, signposted to Belstone. Go through a wooden gate, and where tracks divide turn right onto the path signposted to Skaigh

Woods. This is a rough track running through splendid mature woodland, a little way above the river. Just beyond some new housing there is a small tumbling waterfall by an old mill. There is a hint of things to come, with a hill of bracken, heather and gorse rising up behind the buildings. The pleasant, shaded path alternates between a stony roughness and soft grassland, while the river appears and disappears in its meanderings. The woodland is a constant companion, very colourful when the rhododendron is in bloom, and a small weir serves as a reminder of the centuries' old use of water power. The river itself constantly changes in mood, spreading wide, shallow and clear, dashing down over falls or rushing down narrow, rocky gullies.

One of the overshot waterwheels that were the source of power for the machines of Finch's Foundry.

The path leads down to a wooden footbridge, with a quotation from Henry Williamson's book *Tarka the Otter*, one scene of which was set very near this spot, carved on the handrails. Once across the bridge, the path wanders through woodland paved with mossy boulders, then swings right to a track junction **3** where you turn left towards Belstone. Mature woodland now gives way to scrub with holly, gorse and elder. Ignore a second bridge down to the left and keep to the path that now climbs away from the river, and as it does so the view begins to open out over the moor. Apart from the birds which, unlike the proverbial good little boy, can be heard but not seen, this is also a popular haunt for butterflies. All the time, the scenery is getting more and more rugged with little craggy outcrops erupting through the hillside, where ferns find a footing in seemingly absurdly small cracks and niches. Emerging from the woods and passing between banks of gorse, the buildings of Belstone can be seen up ahead looking out over a broad, grassy slope. Now the path begins to climb much more steeply and over to the left there are splendid views across to the tors that the walk will soon be visiting. The path reaches the rim of the valley and levels out, and you make your way across the grass to the houses and the road.

At the road **4** turn left, and from here there is another stunning view, this time back over the wooded valley of Belstone Cleeve. Continue on along the surfaced road and turn left, then carry on to the road marked as a dead end. Passing a little row of stone cottages, the road turns sharp left to cross a small stream, then right to end at a metal gate, beyond which a broad track leads out onto the moor **5**. This marks a dramatic change in the walk. Now all is openness, as the track heads off across rough ground dotted with granite boulders and the few gorse bushes, almost the only shrubs able to raise themselves much above ground level in this exposed landscape. The infant River Taw winds away in the valley to the left, and the steep slopes of Belstone Common rear up to the right. With such wide vistas, it is possible to see the turning point of the walk, the rounded rock capped hill of Steeperton Tor some three miles up ahead.

The walking is very easy on this section and soon all signs of habitation are left behind. Sheep and cattle graze far out on the moor, and you are likely to encounter a herd of ponies heading for their own private destinations or grazing on a hillside. Penetrating ever deeper into the moor, a meadow pipit might start up from the grass just in front of you, while overhead the sweet song of the skylark makes a welcome appearance or you might catch the characteristic mew of a high-soaring buzzard. Keep following this track, ignoring a left turn down to the river, until the track begins to peter out with grass growing down the middle. When it starts to swing left **6**, turn right onto a rather faint path leading up the shoulder of the hill on the right. There is no need to worry about keeping to an exact route as there is a very clear landmark to aim for, the rocky outcrop of Oke Tor at the top of the ridge **A**.

On reaching the rocks there is a chance to look around and take in the vastness of Dartmoor, with trees counted in single figures and even the tough gorse unable to rise more than a few inches on the exposed higher ground. Few parts of Britain can seem as lonely as this, but for those who relish wild scenery there are few better places either. The summit rocks show the typical Dartmoor formation, piled up like round cheeses. From here the route ahead can be clearly seen. Leaving the summit rocks on your right, take the path that heads to the right of shapely Steeperton Tor – although this is the next main objective, the route goes past it to find a stream crossing and then doubles back. A broader track is soon joined which passes above the deep gulley on the left. Soon it begins to head downhill to a ford where tongues of spoil lick the hillside, all that remains of a former tin mine **B**. Although this is known as a mine, it was worked by cutting away the hillside rather than by burrowing deep underground. Cross the stream and take the path that climbs for a way but soon levels out at a point where there is an area of considerable bank erosion **7**. Turn back sharp left onto a green track that heads straight up towards the flagpole and observation post on the rocky summit **C**.

When the top is reached, you can enjoy truly panoramic views and you feel as if all Dartmoor is spread out around you, like some great billowing yet frozen sea, where dark rocks have taken the place of white caps of foam. It is also a good place to take a break, since whichever way the wind is blowing you can always get behind the sheltering rocks. The way down takes you back south again, but not along the obvious green path cutting a swathe through the darker heather towards prominent Hangingstone Hill. Instead you take the much less distinct path to the left of it, which once again has a convenient landmark to aim for in the shape of the prominent summit of the aptly named Wild Tor. The path eventually leads down to a crossing place on the little Steeperton Brook **8**. Here you can see the remains of a stone hut, rather crudely built from boulders collected on the moor. It was here, centuries ago, that a tin streamer came to – almost literally – scratch a living.

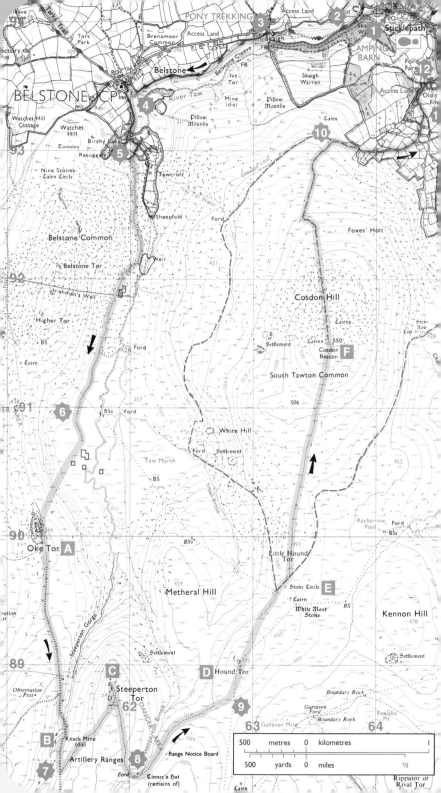

Cross the stream and take the path above the gulley, which follows it for a little way but soon bears away to the right up the hillside, keeping to a line between the rough grassland to the right and the heather-covered slope on the left. This will bring you out onto a much more distinct raised path **9** which heads straight for the summit of Hound Tor **D**. Turn left to follow this track to the summit, which is marked by a cairn. At the top, there is another splendid viewpoint, and the next stage of the walk can be seen as a path wriggling its way down to a stone circle **E**. Take this route down to the circle, which was built in this remote spot some time in the Bronze Age. It is not perhaps too surprising to find these people on Dartmoor, since tin is, with copper, one of the two elements that go to make up bronze, but that gets us no nearer to an understanding of the mysteries of these standing stones, and to add to the puzzle a mighty monolith can be seen out to the right of the path silhouetted against the sky. What religious rites did these Bronze Age communities practise here on the open moor 3000 years ago?

Once again, there is a clear marker for the last climb of the day, the cairn that marks the summit of Cosdon Hill **F**. The route follows the obvious path heading straight uphill, but soon begins to display one of the most irritating characteristics of very rounded hills. The summit itself is soon lost from view, but the path seems to lead on to a horizon just a few hundred metres away. So you put your head down and plod, and when you look up nothing has changed, the top is no nearer. And so it goes on until the cairn and trig point put in an appearance and the long haul is over. Pass the trig point on your left, and now a very different view opens up ahead. It comes as quite a shock after the wide emptiness to look out at a  patchwork of fields and traffic on the distant A30. A small cairn now marks the top of the path down the other side. At first it is a clear, grassy track through heather, and Sticklepath soon comes into view, but the route moves away from it to the right heading off towards the tall church tower of South Tawton. This area is very popular with riders, and the horses have created their own jumble of tracks on the hillside, but there is no real problem as long as you keep the tower as your landmark. Eventually, the way forward will be barred by a wall at the foot of the hill **10**. Turn right at the wall, which is a typically higgledy-piggledy construction of stones, varying in size from rocks you could hold in your hands to monstrous boulders. Such walls were built to last. Follow the wall as it turns round to the left to arrive at a green lane where you turn right. Bird life is prolific here, and if the sweet song of the moorland birds is lost, the brilliant plumage of the chaffinch and bullfinch more than compensates.

At the end of the track, go through the gate to a path junction **11** and turn left onto the path signposted to Ford Cross. Continue down a sunken lane almost totally closed over by trees, then at the next junction turn left onto a lane sunk even deeper into the land, so that the banks rise high above you, so steeply that they have been buttressed by walls. The stones are blanketed in green moss of almost luminescent greenness, creating an eerie effect as if one were sinking down into some strange underworld. It ends at a small stream that bounces along over rocky ledges. The path follows the line of the stream to a little roadway **12** which leads down to the right and the main road. Cross over to the footpath on the far side, and turn left. This is now a pleasant approach back to Sticklepath, past a number of attractive thatched cottages, before the arrival of the bridge over the Taw announces that your walk is about to come to an end.

The green, mysterious depths of the sunken lane that leads the walker back towards Sticklepath.

## Throwleigh

14 miles (23 km)  See map on pages 40 and 41

This offers a complete contrast to the first Sticklepath walk, and is ideal for those days when the tops are lost in cloud. It is a walk of great contrasts incorporating quiet country lanes, riverside strolls and a dramatic route above the deep gorge of the River Teign. It does not start at Sticklepath itself, but 2.5 miles (4 km) away at Throwleigh. You could walk the extra miles, or drive to Throwleigh by taking the main road towards Whiddon Down and turning right on the minor road at South Zeal.

Throwleigh is a delightful spot of good solid stone houses well able to withstand the blasts from the neighbouring moor. The walk starts at the heart of the village marked by a stone cross and the lit-tle village pond **1,** an area with car parking space. Walk up the road to the church, which is unusual in having a thatched lych gate attached to a thatched cottage. A typical Dartmoor granite church with tall tower, it was mostly rebuilt in the fifteenth century, but inside are some twentieth-century oddities. The chancel screen is topped by carved figures from Oberammergau which look dis-tinctly strange in this most English of churches.

Leaving the church, turn right out of the gate to take the minor road up the hill, a typical sunken lane with high banks bearing a colourful display of flowers. Soon the houses of the village are left behind and you reach a point where the road turns sharp right by a splendid old house Higher Shilston **2**. Turn left through the kissing gate to take the path that runs through a farmyard of ducks and geese to continue down the field with the wall to the left. This brings you out to rough moorland dotted with gorse. Go through the gate and take the driveway down to the road where you turn left **3**.

This is a total contrast to the first lane, not enclosed but open to the moor with a gurgling stream for company. The road begins to swing away from the stream, then just before reaching the cattle grid **4** turn right on the footpath signposted The Mariners Way and head through the gap in the gorse down towards the stream crossed by a simple bridge, just a single slab of stone dropped over the water. Once across, turn left then immediately right onto a more distinct path through the gorse. The ground can be muddy, but conveniently placed stones keep you clear of the mire. Join a track passing a farm and come out once again onto a moorland scene of massive boulders and still more gorse. It is a harsh landscape and the gains made by farmers must have been hard won.

At the roadway **5** turn left to reach Moortown crossroads, where you continue straight on. Ted Hughes used the name 'Moortown' for his collection of ferociously earthy poems of North Devon farming life. At the next junction, turn right with expansive moorland views up ahead. As the road turns sharp left **6** carry straight on through the gate to take the footpath to Gidleigh. The path runs through farmland and busy Moortown Brook rushes along beside you. Cross this on another simple stone bridge and go through the smaller of two gates. Carry on down the right hand side of two fields then cross at the next to have the fence on your left. The immediate surroundings are of widespread pasture, but up ahead conifers darken the horizon. Leave this field and continue straight on down the road opposite to Gidleigh.

Once again this is a small village but boasting a handsome church with a tall tower. Rather surprisingly, just before the church you reach a small castle sitting somewhat incongruously in a private garden **A**. The building itself dates from the fourteenth century and is more fortified house than actual fortress. The church is well worth a visit. There is a remarkable set of carved headstones, many dating back to the seventeenth century, lined up against the wall, but the chief glory is inside, a very elaborate painted screen. On leaving the church, continue up the road, which swings left then right to a road junction, where you turn right. A short climb brings you to the edge of the woods **7**, where you turn left onto the broad track above the fields. There is a huge contrast between the vistas of farmland on one side and the glum darkness of close-set conifers on the other. Reaching a large clearing, do not take the obvious forest track, but continue up a much narrower path, marked simply with refreshing brevity 'Path'. This is a most pleasant route at first wandering steadily downhill through heavily-scented pine, but gradually the way steepens, becoming ever more stony, until at the end it is a natural staircase of rock. All the time a roar of water can be heard from the valley floor. At the foot of the hill you come out onto a wide track where you turn right and the river comes into view. This is the northern arm of the Teign, a river which will dominate much of the walk, and here it is at its liveliest, leaping and bounding on its way down from the moor.

Where the river is temporarily lost from view, look out for a turning on the left, again just signposted as 'Path' which takes you

The footbridge across the North Teign River, as it rushes through the woods below Gidleigh Tor.

down to a footbridge **B** for the first really close look at this beautiful river valley, where broadleaved trees hang their branches low over the dashing waters. There is a steep little climb up from the bridge. On reaching the top, turn right along the edge of the wood, then left to reach a road where you turn left and immediately right to continue on the path. This is a pleasant grassy track with a tangle of overgrown woodland to the right. At the next track junction **8** turn left onto a path sunk deep between high banks and worn down by ages of use to the bedrock. At the end of

this steep descent turn left then right at the road and we have now joined the Two Moors Way long distance footpath. Apart from the usual flowered banks this is an area which seems particularly attractive to birds, from busy little wrens to perpetually bobbing wagtails, and there are extensive views of a landscape neatly parcelled out into small square fields.

Where the road turns sharp right **9** carry straight on along the bridleway. Once again a gentle descent steepens and again the path bites deep into the land to create a stony gully. After reaching a hollow followed by a short climb the view changes quite dramatically. Now woodland and gorse creep up on the right while the bank to the left is buttressed by a massive stone wall. The path takes a respite with a little wriggle and squirm before the final steep descent to the road. Continue straight on along the road and now the South Teign appears on the right, about to join its northern neighbour. Cross this river at Leigh Bridge and look out for the restored Leigh Cross **C** on a rocky outcrop on the right. This section is full of contrasts: a manicured garden drops down to the river while at the roadside immense beech trees have established themselves on the bank and clasp it firmly with claw-like roots; near at hand is ordered farmland, beyond that the wild moor. Holy Street Manor appears, mightily impressive but almost entirely rebuilt in the early twentieth century. A small stream joins in on the left running between carefully constructed stone walls, which suggest it might be a mill leat, and sure enough the ruins of a former woollen mill appear by the next crossroads, just beyond the kennels.

At the crossroads **10** turn left to cross the bridge over the mill stream, continue on over the triple-arched Chagford Bridge and turn right onto the riverside path. The river will now be a close companion for a couple of miles or so and it will appear in many different moods, spreading wide and placid or squeezed into a narrow gorge to rush over falls. Dippers can be seen on rocks and there is a chance of catching the sudden blue flash as a kingfisher darts across the water. That increasingly widespread immigrant the Canada goose is a regular visitor. At first this is what one could call calm walking over grassland that softens the way with no navigational problems to worry about. The village of Chagford can be seen across the water, then, after crossing a couple of tributary streams, the route runs through an oak wood. Now a weir provides a noisy interruption to the river's gentle flow and the path continues along the leat that runs from above the dam. The mill it once served is still some way ahead.

Stay with the leat then cross it by a footbridge and take the path beside the hedge. Go through a gap in the hedge and cross the field to the stile by the river **11** where you turn left onto the road.

There is a temporary diversion from the river which has gone away for a wander. The road arrives, rather surprisingly, by a large open air swimming pool, just beyond which is the long expected mill. Turn right through a farmyard and cross a stile for another gentle riverside stroll. The landscape is becoming more uneven with little oak-topped knolls and soon a stile leads to woodland where oak trees are surrounded by a jumble of mossy boulders through which you pick your way. A watery roar announces the arrival of yet another weir, and where the path divides by an immense oak keep following the riverside walk down to the main road at Dogmarsh bridge. Cross straight over the road to the gate opposite which admits you to the National Trust's Drogo Estate.

The path still keeps by the river but now there is a promise of a much more dramatic landscape up ahead with high hills and craggy outcrops. Then as the river begins to swing to the left you get a first glimpse of Castle Drogo **D** on its airy perch. Built between 1910 and 1930 to the design of Sir Edwin Lutyens it combines a stern uncompromising exterior with a comfortable home tucked snugly away inside. Enter the woods, then just before reaching the foot-bridge turn left to head uphill, signposted to Hunters Path **12**. The route climbs past a traditional but very grand Devon farmhouse and a no less attractive cottage with a huge external chimney. The way uphill continues by road with a closer view of the castle.

Where the trees clear on the right **13** turn sharply back onto a path that begins to work its way round the shoulder of the hill. This part of the walk is very popular and justly famous and it soon becomes clear why this is so. As the path bends so the view begins to improve. First there is the magnificent sight of the deep, wooded cleft where just a glitter of reflected light indicates the presence of the River Teign far below. It might seem that the view could not get more dramatic, but there is still better up ahead. The path occupies a narrow ledge near the top of the hill and there are various signposted paths to the left for anyone wishing to visit the castle, otherwise keep straight on enjoying these splendid views. The crux of the high drama comes when you reach the shattered rocks that top Sharp Tor and only the most drearily unromantic could resist the temptation to stop here for a while and simply take it all in. There is a second craggy viewpoint, beyond which the grandeur diminishes and you should start to look out for a turning on the left, where little log steps lead to a path to Drewsteignton **14**.

The drama is over for a while as the path follows a gorse hedge beside lush meadows bright with buttercups, daisies and fleabane. Up ahead is Drewsteignton with the inevitable tall church tower to signal its presence. Now the view is all of farmland not moor and in the distance the A30 can be seen cutting its way through an intricate maze of old lanes. Continue down the field to the edge of the wood where you turn right then left over a stile. Wooden steps take you steeply downhill through the trees with, discouragingly, an all too clear view of an equally steep hill immediately ahead. At the foot of the hill where tracks meet turn left on the bridleway for Drewsteignton to begin the climb. Reaching the road **15** you can turn right into the village with its well known old thatched pub the Drewe Arms or turn left to continue the walk.

The New Stone Age burial chamber known as Spinsters' Rock, originally built some 4500 years ago but reconstructed in the last century.

For the next four or so miles we shall be staying with peaceful country lanes, where hedgerows offer a seemingly endless variety of blooms from the pallor of white bryony and stitchwort to the deeper shades of vetch and dog-violet. Add to these the ever present bird life and even when the wider vistas are closed off there is no way one could ever get bored in such scenery. At the road junction **16** where this road swings away to the left carry straight on along an even more minor road – one of those lanes so little used that grass grows up the middle. There is now a long, very steady climb through farmland with a backdrop of moor and the view constantly enlarges until, on reaching the top, a richly varied landscape is spread out all around you. Carry on past a right turn, followed by two left turns very close together and pass under power lines to a division in the road **17** where you turn left on the road signposted to Spinsters' Rock.

There are still wide views to enjoy and just beyond the next hill, the Spinsters' Rock can be seen in a field on the left by the farm. This is a New Stone Age burial chamber, stripped of its earth covering, so that it now looks like a giant's stool with a vast capstone supported on upright slabs. The curious name derives from a story that when the stones collapsed in 1862 they were re-erected one day before break-fast by three spinsters – and pretty hefty spinsters they must have been! As you approach the main road, a stout upstanding parade of beech provide a guard of honour. Cross straight over and take the minor road opposite towards Gidleigh. Now there is another long, steady climb through very attractive farmland where, in what is now sadly all too rare a sight, the fields are spangled with flowers.

At the road junction by Monks Withecombe Farm **18** turn right back towards Throwleigh. Carry straight on at the next crossroads towards the communications mast and there is another change of mood. Now the route is tree shaded and the road opens up to the right to an area of rough moor blanketed in bracken. Beyond that the road plunges downhill and continues to descend past the road junc-tion. Eventually you arrive at the stream at the bottom. Here the road divides **19** and you keep to the right, still heading for Throwleigh. There is a vicious little climb, though you may well have chaffinches to offer you vocal encouragement. The climb leads past the rather forlorn old village school and the plain but neat Methodist chapel to reach a T-junction **20.** Turn left and then almost immediately right beside a cottage to join a rough track marked as not suitable for motor vehicles. The walk ends with this bridleway where the trees meet overhead that will take you back to the centre of the village.

# Peter Tavy

This unassuming little village sits at the western edge of Dartmoor, which rises so steeply above it that you have scarcely left the houses behind before you have reached the moor at its wildest. It has two essentials of the best Dartmoor villages, a church with a soaring tower dating from around 1500 and an almost equally ancient inn.

## WALK 1 | White Tor and Mary Tavy
10 miles (16 km) See map on pages 48 and 49

The first part of this walk takes you far out onto the moor, while the return includes a visit to one of the most important industrial archaeological sites in the area. Please note that this walk enters the Merrivale Firing Range, so it is essential to check that no firing is taking place before setting out.

Take the road out of the village passing the church **1** on the left. After a short climb, turn right at the first junction onto the road marked as a dead end that heads straight up towards the open moor. The road climbs between banks brightened by stitchwort and campion, then where the road turns sharp right **2**, carry straight on up the face of the hill. Extensive views open out and include Brent Tor, the curious conical hill topped by a church over to the left. Cross a small bank and ditch, part of the boundary of an ancient field system, and the path appears as a pale streak in the bracken, heading up past a solitary hawthorn. As you climb, a jumble of rocks comes into view, marking the summit of the hill and the route lies just to the right of these. All the time the view is widening to include distant hills and tors. Walking along the summit ridge, you will see a wall and a path coming in from the left. Now everything converges, and the walls squeeze in from either side to form a little lane, with a view of the higher hills and the wide expanse of moor to the north. The lane makes a brief interlude, for everything soon opens out again.

Continue on the obvious track with the wall to the left, and soon that too turns away and all that remains is a track heading away into a wide expanse of moor stretching to the horizon. A solitary stone on a plinth **A** stands beside the track. Carved with a letter 'S' it marks 'Stephen's Grave' though the story behind it seems to have been lost. A short way beyond the stone the track divides **3**. The walk could be continued by following the track straight ahead, but a much more interesting variation is to be made by turning to the left to head for the rocks of White Tor. The track peters out among the clitter near the summit, and here there are traces of circling walls from an Iron Age hill fort **B**. The summit rocks provide a splendid viewpoint overlooking the wide spaces of the moor and even across into Cornwall and the distant bulk of Bodmin Moor. Having left the wide track it now has to be rejoined.

The summit is also an army observation post for the firing range, and a red flag is flown here when the range is in use. Leave the summit passing the little army hut and you will see a standing stone **C** beside the path down below, which is the next landmark. The way down follows no specific path, but passes small cairns of piled stones to reach a humpy, bumpy landscape as if the earth had erupted in a rather unpleasant rash. Having reached the stone, it can be seen as part of a little complex which we can only assume had ritual significance. The single menhir is most impressive and it

The summit of White Tor, which was encircled by stone walls in the Iron Age to create a lonely fortress high above the moor.

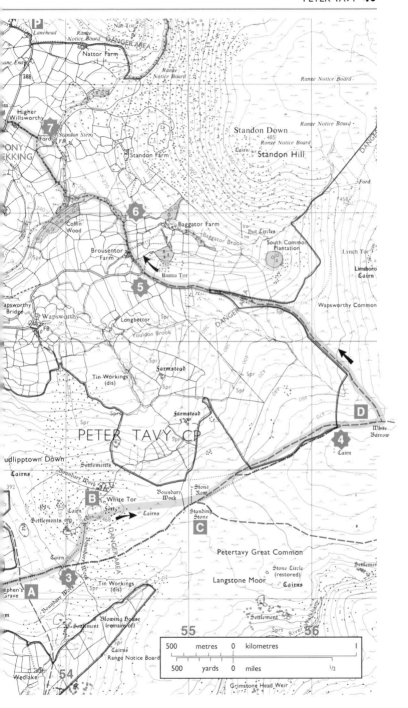

stands at the end of a row of smaller, almost imperceptible stones. Monuments such as this were constructed on many parts of the moor in the Bronze Age – and an even more spectacular example will be met on the next walk.

From here, the way ahead is quite indistinct for a time, but continues on the same line as the track – and there is no need to feel alarmed at the emptiness ahead for it all becomes clear quite soon. Up ahead, a blip appears on the skyline, which in fact marks the end of a stone wall which is the next objective. Paths on the ground are, at best, vague but as you climb the gentle slope the wall duly becomes clearer and you join the obvious path beside it. Where the wall swings away left **4** keep straight on along the track heading towards a large mound **D**. This is White Barrow, another survivor from the Bronze Age, this time a lonely burial mound, and its position was obviously chosen with care, for it would be seen on the skyline by the people who lived in the settlement to the south. From here one looks forward to the wilds of the central moor where tors give a ragged edge to the horizon.

It is now time to turn back, taking a rather vague path that heads at an angle of roughly 45° from the track that has been followed thus far. Coming over the shoulder of the hill, with comfortable walking on bouncy turf, the wall comes into view again and this time head for the right hand end of it. Follow it round as it heads downhill, still enjoying comfortable walking over soft grass. After a time, a second wall comes in from the right to form a drift that leads down to the gate, a funnel effect useful for rounding up sheep and cattle when they have to be brought down off the moor. There are still great views, this time looking out across to Cornwall, while the obvious track leads past the rocks of little Bagga Tor. There is a steady descent through patches of gorse until the path meets the road **5**. Turn off to the right onto the grassy track heading towards the farm which peeps out from its shelter of trees. Follow the rough, tree shaded lane then turn right down the farm approach road, which now heads steeply downhill between stone walls. At the foot of the hill **6** turn left to cross a stile to head downhill with a fence to your right. Once over the next field you come close to the stream and follow it round, while a fine woodland clings precariously to the hill on the left. This brings you down to a footbridge which you do *not* cross, but continue on to stepping stones that first cross the stream then lead on to a second set across the infant River Tavy. At this point if the river is exceptionally high you may be forced to use the bridge. In which case, follow the alternative waymarked route on the permissive path, which will rejoin this route a little further on.

Once across the river, turn right onto the obvious shaded path round the edge of the field, which brings you out by a pair of stiles. Continue up the lane between gorse banks and the wall. At the top of the hill, turn diagonally right to a stile **7** where the two routes are reunited and turn left to follow the edge of the rough moorland. At the road **8** turn left. The road turns right and then sharp left to reach a T-junction, where you turn right. There is a short climb before this wayward road turns sharp left, where you turn off to take the path on the right **9**. Now a little lane leads back up towards the rougher land of gorse and coarse grasses and soon you are back on open access land. Head away from the wood on the left to go uphill towards tracks on the upper level. Where the tracks converge, go through the gate to follow the deep artificial feeder channel rushing down towards the reservoir. Cross over the feeder by the bridge and sluice gates which control the flow to this oddly linear reservoir known as Wheal Jewell **E** – the name 'Wheal' is used in the south west for mines, and there is ample evidence of disturbed ground.

Pass the head of the reservoir and cross the obvious approach road that runs beside it to take a track that heads off in the direction of the low hill on the far side of the main road. The more obvious track is soon left behind for a fainter path through the gorse, with the deep gullies of old workings down to the left. Soon the next landmark comes into view, the engine house of Wheal Betsy **F** and now it is a simple matter of following the path round the hillside to reach it. The mine produced lead and zinc and a considerable amount of silver. It had a chequered history. The old mine workings of uncertain age were reopened in 1806 as Wheal Betsy, closed again and restarted once more, this time as Prince Arthur Consols. As well as the steam engine used for pumping, there were once five water wheels on the site, which was finally abandoned in 1870. The engine house is now in the care of the National Trust.

From the engine house, a clear track leads down to the valley floor, past old spoil heaps and a filled in shaft. From here, turn left up the farm approach road, and continue on the rough track beyond the gate. This swings away to the left and once through the next gate you are back on open land and you follow the path round to the right beside the wall. This leads to a lane **10** running between flowery banks to the road. Turn right to continue down-

The engine house of Wheal Betsy, once home to a mighty steam engine used to pump water from the mine workings.

hill. Just before reaching farm buildings, cross a stone stile on the right **11** to join the footpath beside the stream. There is now a relaxing stroll across the fields to Mary Tavy with a small diversion away from the stream to avoid a marshy area. Then the path turns to cross a footbridge by the houses and continues on the opposite bank of the stream to the road **12**. Turn left over the road bridge, passing another confused area of shafts and spoil heaps, and continue on the dead end road signposted to the church. The church itself reverses the village name, Tavy St Mary – a typical tall-towered building with, rather uncharitably, a set of stocks in the porch.

Where the road ends continue straight on the bridleway to Peter Tavy which heads down a shady lane to the river, running through an attractive wooded valley. Cross over for a gentle climb past rocky outcrops to a sweetly scented finale between high banks on the path that leads back to the centre of the village.

## WALK 2 — Merrivale

11 miles (17.5 km)  See map on pages 56 and 57

Once again, this is a walk over the open access land of the moor, taking in rocky tors and wooded valleys. Do not worry if you see red flags flying along the way – the walk does not encroach on the range.

From the village centre take the road that runs uphill past the village hall. It soon begins to climb steeply between banks and walls, and where it levels out look on the left for stone steps climbing the wall to a stile **1**. Cross over and head across the field to a second stone stile, carry on again over the next field then head for the far left corner eventually leaving by a gate for the short track down to the road. Turn left and follow the road round, still going up hill and where it levels out before reaching the houses **2** turn left through the gate onto a grassy bridleway heading straight up the hill. The farm track swings off to the left but the route carries straight on by the bridlepath sign to climb up beside the gorse, with views to the left over to the rocky summit of Smeardon Down. Walls briefly cut off the view, then it all opens out again and the surroundings become notably more rugged, with boulders dotting the fields and rock outcrops bursting through the surface of the land. Keep on with the wall on the right to reach a gate that leads onto rougher moorland and head towards a signpost on the skyline to the left of the rocks. The path rounds the knoll with its crown of stunted trees to reach the minor road and the open moor.

Cross over the road, and once again this is access land with no clear path. Turn half left away from the road, heading slightly up and around the shoulder of the hill, aiming roughly for the point where the slope of the hill you are climbing meets the slope of the tor behind it. As you work your way round the hill more and more of the next ridge comes into view and you see a pile of rocks on the top looking like a particularly eccentric set of Tudor chimney pots. Looking down into the valley on the left, you can see fields spreading high up the valley.

Once you have the whole ridge in view you can set your sights on the tor at the far right. Your route will bring you down past a little settlement, probably Bronze Age, consisting of an enclosure with the typical low circular walls of the old, rough houses **A**. From here head up the hill to the rocks at the head of the ridge, Great

Staple Tor **B**. From this splendid viewpoint you can look down on the wanderings of the Tavy and the Tamar as they unite on their way to the sea. This is a great place just to sit among the rocks to admire the scenery or watch the whirling ravens who have made their homes among these rocks. For the descent, head towards the buildings of Merrivale on the road, passing the quarry with its great jib crane, showing sad signs of disuse.

On reaching the road **3** cross over and turn left along the little grassy footpath, passing the quarry spoil heaps held in place by a really massive retaining wall of immense granite blocks. Stay with the road as it dips to cross the river, then where the wall comes to an end on the right, turn up onto the moor away from the road and head off towards a very obvious landmark, the tall communication mast on the horizon. This line will bring you past one of the mysterious sites that are such a feature of the region **C**. There are three stone rows, two double and one single, the one nearest the road containing over 150 small stones. Nearby, and all part of the same complex, are cairns, standing stones and a stone circle. The site dates back to the Bronze Age, but it is also known as Plague Market, for it was here that traders met when plague was ravaging Tavistock. Perhaps some old sense of this being a sacred site made it seem all the safer.

The next objective can be seen up ahead, the farm below the mast. Cross the stream at the obvious ford and the path now climbs past the walls of an old enclosure to go up to the left of the farm to join a wide track passing behind it **4**. Turn right onto what was once a tramway, a railed track used by horse-drawn waggons serving the quarries. These were once worked by the inmates of the nearby prison at Princetown, and the quarry spoil heaps are now a prominent feature up ahead. Along the way you will see some of the stone sleeper blocks, still carrying the indentations of the rails. The route passes the high granite faces, now mainly of interest to rock climbers practising their art. Keep following the old tramway until it reaches a T-junction **5**. Turn right onto a track having an even more pronounced railway look to it. This is all that remains of the Plymouth and Dartmoor Railway, built like the tramway for use by horses and opened to link the quarries to Sutton Harbour in 1823.

Just below the next spoil heaps on the hillside, look for a wooden gate on the left with a bridlepath sign **6**. From here a steep path leads down to the little valley. It winds down through rocks to a gap in the wall, where it heads off to the right through scrubby woodland. It is a little indistinct in places, but blue-topped posts act as waymarkers.

One of the mysteries of Dartmoor: the stone rows marching across the moor near Merrivale were erected in the Bronze Age.

After making your way through this confusion of stunted trees and boulders you follow the line of the wall on the right down to a stream, crossed by a little agile stone stepping. You emerge near a cottage, enjoying a most enviable situation, and after a little more maze threading you reach the cottage approach drive, which leads you down to the road. Now the view changes very markedly as you

look down into a deep wooded valley. At the road, carry straight on, over the crossroads, for a steep descent to the woods. Having reached the river, there is the inevitable climb up the other side.

Once clear of the wood, turn right by the cattle grid **7** to take an old lane that goes straight up the hill to emerge at the road by a grand house, Stoneycroft. Turn off immediately to the right onto the path next to the house entrance, climbing once more through mature woodland, where mighty beech lord it over the lesser trees. The lane ends at a field where you follow the path round to the left to cross a ladder stile with a spectacular view out over the woods to moor and tor. Next bear left towards another stile, then follow a diagonal across the next fields to head towards another patch of moor. A short lane now leads down to the road, where you turn right to reach a little road junction before heading off up the hill. Again, any route can be taken – the shortest passes to the left of the cottage halfway up the hill to reach the rocks at the top of Pew Tor. This offers the last of the grand panoramas of this walk, and a chance to renew acquaintance with the tors already met along the way.

Now take the obvious track that swings round to the left to join the road, where you turn right **8**. The road soon swings away from the moor, still going downhill, but now passing through a land-scape of small fields and patches of wood, with just the occasional hint of rough grass and heather here and there. The quiet road enjoys the accompaniment of some majestic horse chestnut and a little gurgly stream. At the road junction **9** turn right and the famil-iar hill of Brent Tor appears up ahead. Keep following this route round to the right to cross over the B-road to take the minor road to Peter Tavy. At the next road junction **10** turn right onto the dead end road to Collaton. At the top of the road turn left by the farm, then left again through a gate for the path to Sowtontown. The path runs at first with the wall on the left, then crosses to the other side, still heading in the same direction. Once over the farm approach road, the path carries straight on across the fields by a series of gates and stiles until it reaches the road **11**.

Turn right at the road, then left at the next junction and the encouraging sight of Peter Tavy church appears not so very far ahead. At the next road junction, turn right and the road dips down to a stream. Just beyond that **12** turn left onto the bridleway and head off towards the top right hand corner of the field to join a track which leads straight onto the road which is followed back to the start.

# Buckfastleigh

Set down beneath the wooded slopes of the moor, Buckfastleigh is a pleasant, unpretentious town that developed around the woollen industry. This give it a very different character from its neighbour Buckfast, based on the Abbey founded in the eleventh century. It was destroyed in Henry VIII's reign, but was reborn in 1882. A new monastery was built by French Benedictines and it remains in use. And for those whose legs get a little weary there is a chance to view the Dart valley while being hauled by steam locomotive on the South Devon Railway.

## WALK 1 — Buckfastleigh and Scorriton

12 miles (19.5 km)  See map on pages 64 and 65

A walk that starts in the wooded valley, it reaches nearly 2000 ft (610 m) up on the open moor among the remains of old tin workings.

From the town centre go up Chapel Street, with a curious set of buildings on the left consisting of conventional cottages, but with a weatherboarded upper storey running right across the row. The name Tenterloft Cottages gives the clue. This is where woollen cloth was stretched out to dry suspended on tenterhooks. The chapels appear next, one rather grim and dour, the other soberly classical, followed by a Catholic church. Where the main road bends right, carry straight on up Jordan Street and along the road marked as a dead end. This heads straight into a little lane bordered by stone walls. The River Mardle can be heard but not seen over to the right. The view briefly opens up to a landscape of fields and woods, before being lost again as the track drops down between high banks and hedges. Beyond Merryfield Farm you can see the attractive woodland that marks the course of the river. Cross a stream and then opposite the entrance to Wotton Farm **1** turn right at the gate to take the obvious footpath heading into the wood.

Cross the stream and head off towards the craggy hillside. Continue on at the first track junction and follow the path as it swings to the left through oak woodland, dotted with rock outcrops with a stream to the left. The track climbs to the edge of the wood, where your nostrils are assailed by the pungent smell of wild garlic. The path

A panoramic view from the walk near Scorriton, showing the changes on the landscap

patterns of neat fields gives way to open moorland.

continues to climb up a shaded lane to the road **2** where you turn left. This is another typical lane of high bank and hedge, but up ahead is a tempting glimpse of moorland and tor. At the next junction **3** turn left onto the Holne road, heading off towards a smoothly-rounded wooded hill like a plumped-up green cushion, and now all the surrounding hills come into view. At the next crossroads the view gets even better, and someone has thoughtfully provided a seat so that it can be enjoyed in comfort. Carry straight on now on the Scorriton road. This road has very little traffic, though you may be passed by the local tourist transport, a trap drawn by two ponies.

At the edge of the woodland **4** turn right up the track past Burchetts Lodge that takes you steadily uphill along the edge of the wood. The old boundary is marked by a bank, topped by a procession of stately beech trees. Where the track divides go straight on into the wood, a very pleasant stroll, especially in Spring when the bluebells are in flower. Once over the top of the hill you meet a second track and turn left to keep to the edge of the wood. This is a splendidly varied walk, with mature trees, a harmonious bird chorus, occasionally interrupted by the harsh discordance of a jay, while beyond the edge of the wood the presence of the stream is hinted at by a meadow brightened by water iris. As the stream comes into view, the trees by the path have grown so close together that their branches have become intertwined, so that it is impossible to tell where one tree ends and the next starts. A small ruined building **A** contains bearings for a water wheel, and sure enough an old leat appears beside the path.

On leaving the wood, cross the footbridge **5** over the clear-watered stream and go on up the hill to the farm – and any doubt about the interpretation of the ruins is dispelled by its name, Mill Leat Farm. Immediately beyond the stone barn, turn left onto the footpath signposted to Holne. Now there is a really grand prospect of moorland ahead of you. The path keeps to a comparatively low level on the slope above the hedge with its wide sprawling oak. Cross a stile to continue on a more obvious path through rough grassland, and having left the rowdy jay back in the wood, you now have to endure raucous pheasants. The path dips then swings right to go uphill and the next objective, Scorriton, can be seen on the left. At the road **6** turn left to go downhill, passing a beautiful old farm with an imposing stone-arched entrance. At the road junction turn right **7** down the very narrow road that heads down between high banks to the village. On reaching Scorriton turn right at the war memorial onto the Holne road passing alternative sources of refreshment – the village pump and the village pub.

Leaving the village, the moor itself can be seen not so far away, but there are also delights closer at hand. You drop down to the river valley between banks rich in flowers, where delicate pinkish red campion stand out against patches of white stitchwort – and look out for an old grinding mill by the roadside which has been reused as an unusual flower container. Then the road turns right for the hamlet of Michelcombe with the moor rising steeply from its back door. Surprisingly, at this height, an orchard has been planted and has thrived and a house of brick and timber strikes an odd note among the ubiquitous granite, as if someone had transplanted a small patch of Kent.

Go on to the bridge **8** and turn left on the road marked as a bridleway. Where the tarmac ends the rough track immediately divides and you take the route to the left climbing up towards the moor. This is a wide, rough track on the fringe of the farmland, where coarse grass, gorse and bracken invade the pasture. A steady, long climb brings gradual changes: the tall trees are left behind and the few that manage to retain a foothold struggle to raise their heads against the wind, and soon only the sturdy thorn survive. Then track and walls end and there is just the open moor ahead of you.

There are two obvious tracks, both of which you ignore and instead head straight on forward up the hill, and as you climb the way ahead becomes clearer. Patches of gorse appear among thorn trees and the path can be seen as a grassy way through the bracken – just how clear it is will depend on the time of year. In any case, there is soon confirmation that you are on the right line when you reach a simple stone bridge over a stream. Now there is a comfortable grass track with gorse to the left, which soon gives way to a sandy path, and you are indeed on Sandy Way. The route continues to a plateau with a rather flattened out cairn **9** where you turn left onto a track lined with marker stones. This is very much the lonely moor, with meadow pipits among the few visible inhabitants. Looking back to the right you can see a reservoir down in the valley, and soon the land beside the walk is gouged out into deep gullies **B**. These are the workings of the old tin streamers who dug their way down to the layers of ore – often in the form of fragments no bigger than pebbles – and followed the course down the hillside. Now it is a jumble of spoil heaps and crevasses.

The path climbs more gently now with mining remains still prominent over to the right. Just before reaching the prominent

humps on the skyline turn left **10** onto the clear track running parallel to the ridge. Since leaving Buckfastleigh you will now have climbed nearly 1500 ft (450 m) to reach this airy walk across the high moor. It is a short visit, for now you will be able to see the valley that marks the route back down. A path leads off to the left **11** heading for a rock-strewn gully. It soon becomes indistinct, and the easiest route to follow is on the high ground to the right of the gully. You aim for the spot where a wider gully comes in from the right. This will bring you down to a stream, where a path runs across a ford, and once across, swings away from the stream to the right. Now you look down on the farmland on the lower slopes. Eventually you arrive at the remains of an old walled enclosure and ruined buildings, all that is left of a homestead abandoned many centuries ago **C**. Now you have another landmark to head for, a hill up ahead topped with gorse with a wooded hill beyond it. Soon you reach a clearer path heading to the point where the infant River Mardle disappears into the trees.

A pleasant turf path winds down through woods to cross a brook via convenient boulders, and you follow the stream downhill until you reach a footbridge on the left **12**. Cross over and take the stony path beside the fence. This attractive route with grand views of moor stretching to the horizon climbs up through gorse to another stream crossing. Here is a steep little climb up a grassy track, followed by a little dip into a hollow. The path climbs again past a newly planted patch of conifers, then where the wall turns to the left **13** follow it round to a signpost at the end of the bridleway to Cross Furzes. No route-finding problems here – it is rather like leaving a maze of country roads to join a motorway.

This wide track leads you down to a minor road **14** where you turn right for the return to Buckfastleigh. This is a pleasant, quiet road with constantly changing views. At first there is a mixture of moor and pasture, then the rougher ground gives way to a smoothly rounded hill enlivened with gorse. Then as with all Devon lanes, there is a period where it sinks down between bank and hedge. The road passes a large area of woodland and the busy world returns as you look down on the traffic on the A38. Carry straight on at the road junction for a steep descent down yet another deep lane. Buckfastleigh is now very close, but remains hidden from view. Even when the first houses appear, the route keeps its secretive nature diving down into a deep rock cutting from which you only emerge when you reach the town.

## South Brent and Dean Moor

13 miles (21 km)  See map on pages 70 and 71

This walk begins at South Brent, roughly five miles from Buckfastleigh and most of the route lies out on the moor. It is particularly rugged and wild at the northern end, which may make walking a little more difficult than when following nice, clear paths but gives the whole trip its very special character.

The starting point is South Brent church **1** on the northern edge of the village, and those arriving by car will find adequate parking near the railway bridge. The church itself has a rather stumpy tower, a modest affair compared with the lofty majority of Dartmoor churches, but compensates with a grand, airy interior. From here take the dead end road that leads under the railway viaduct and ends at a kissing gate and a riverside path This is a very enjoyable start with the River Avon running fast and shallow through woodland that culminates in a splendid display of wide spreading horse chestnut and no less imposing beech. The path ends at the road **2** where you turn right and immediately left towards Lutton.

The deep lane climbs steadily at first, then where it begins to level out and swing to the right look out for a stile on the left which leads to the footpath to Lutton **3**. Once over the stile turn right towards the next stile and carry on towards a house with a sumptuous copper beech. You leave the path by cottages and a delightful stone house with a 'green man' over the doorway. Continue up to the road and turn left to join the broad, stony bridleway. Cross a stream on a simple, stone slab bridge and continue through the right-hand of two gates. Soon you begin to climb and the track narrows down to a shady lane, still following the Avon, out of sight but not out of hearing, among the trees on the left. This long climb continues through farmland with views out over the moor. The fields to the side get steadily rougher, with patches of gorse and bracken and there are occasional incursions into copses. Then, rather surprisingly, the path levels out and there is a return to lush fields surrounded by pine.

Cross over a stream to reach the road and continue straight across on the footpath to Shipley Bridge. You go through a farmyard to reach a path bounded by stone walls and overhung by trees. There is a stiff little climb at the top of which is a little bench with a good view, to provide an excuse for getting your breath back. Cross a stile for a pleasant walk along the fringe of a wood, which in Spring is a mass of bluebells, and the tors of Brent Moor appear up ahead. After all that climbing, the path suddenly heads downhill to a stream and the road where you turn left. This brings you to what is now a car park, but was originally an industrial site **A**. There were, in fact, two industries here. In 1844 two Plymouth industrialists, Peter Adams and Jacob Hall Drew began a works for producing naphtha, an inflammable oil, from peat taken higher up the moor, and the same site was also used for the storage of china clay from the not very successful local works.

From the car park, you turn right onto the bridleway, signposted as Abbot's Way, which is also the private road to the Avon Dam. The river bumps along beside you, dashing through deep rocky gorges, overhung by sessile oak. Some of the trees have immense root systems that engulf whole mossy boulders. The river is constantly changing, sometimes tumbling over flat slabs of rock, then widening to dark, treacly-brown pools. After crossing the bridge, the scenery begins to change as you come out onto the open moor with its grazing sheep and cattle with the steep, bracken slopes of Brent Moor to the left. Where the road swings left, following the line of the stream **4** turn right onto the rough, unsurfaced track. On the left is the deep Zeal Gulley and to the right the broken down walls of an old settlement. The track climbs up past the high stone wall of the Avon Dam, crossing the line of an old constructors' rail track.

The path now becomes quite indistinct. At first you follow the edge of the reservoir, but do not follow it round to the left. Continue along the flank of the stone littered hillside with the small stream down to your left, cutting through pallid, reedy grass. A more obvious path cuts across in front of you **5**. Turn left onto this path which is part of the Abbot's Way, and cross the stream at an obvious ford. This is exhilarating walking now as the track develops into a grassy path across the moor with the reservoir down to the right. Even this high on the moor, long-horned cattle graze looked down on by buzzards effortlesly riding the thermals and by hovering kestrel. It seems an empty land, but old stone walls to the right tell a story of former settlements. An odd conical hill pops up briefly above the skyline – and will reappear later in the walk. Once the reservoir has been left behind, the path becomes indistinct again, but takes a line roughly following the stream, carv-

A simple clapper bridge crosses a stream in the lonely heart of the moor below Huntingdon Warren.

ing a sinuous way across the hill. Little streams course down the slope and the walker has to take whatever crossing seems easiest. A reassuring marker to your path appears by the widest of the streams, the crudely carved Huntingdon Cross **B**. The land to the right is Huntingdon Warren, where men built up sandy hills known as pillow mounds as homes for rabbits – not out of any kindness of heart but with a view to tasty rabbit pies. Keep with the stream as it swings round to the left and follow it round to reach a clapper bridge, made by laying stone slabs onto rough piers made of piles of stones **6**.

Cross the bridge and follow the stream back in the direction you have just come for 700-1000 ft (2-300 m) until you reach a

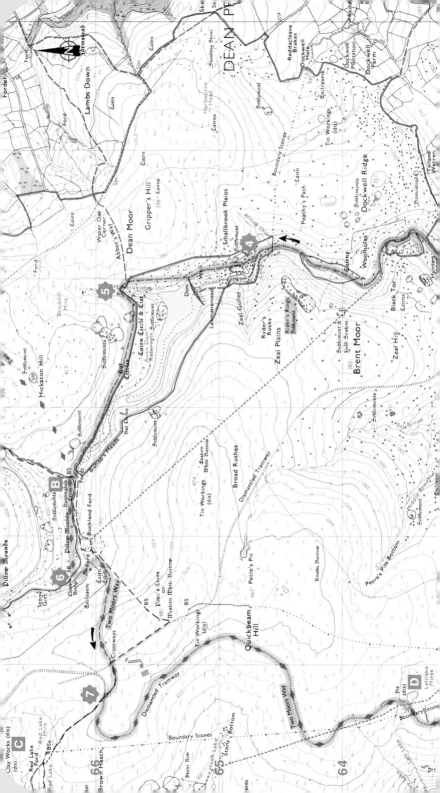

grassy clearing with a small circle of broken stones. The next part sounds complicated but works out easily in practice. A rough gully runs up the hill on the right with a suggestion of a path beside it. Follow this and a deeper gully appears on the left and you continue uphill taking a line between the two. As you climb, the conical hill **C** seen earlier on the walk comes into view and a small stone building is silhouetted on the skyline. There is no obvious path, but if you aim for somewhere between these two landmarks you will come to the top of the ridge where all will be made clear. In front of you is a broad green track running from the 'hill' to curve away across the moor. What you are seeing is the spoil heap from the old Red Lane china clay works, while the track is all that remains of a 3ft gauge tramway which linked the works to the main line railway at Bittaford.

Where you join the old tramway **7** – the exact point does not matter – turn left to follow it as it sweeps round the hillside. Apart from the high mound of the spoil heap this seems almost featureless moorland, and without this track to follow, route-finding would be quite problematical. The land is a gentle series of undulations, grass-covered hills with colours ranging from green to palest straw and patched with heather. But as the path swings round the hill in a great bend so the view changes very dramatically and rocky tors erupt on the skyline, while gullies chart the course of old tin workings. Gradually the track straightens out to head in a generally southerly direction and you begin to see the fringe of the moor and its pattern of small fields. A small lake and spoil heaps **D** mark the site of an old mine and one of the few surviving structures from the old line puts in an appearance in the form of a bridge, built on the skew with the bricks under the arch laid in diagonals. The route is now following the line of a ridge, and you can look down to the right to a deepening river valley and patches of woodland. Being an old railway the track keeps more or less to a level making for easy walking over the moor with plenty of time to enjoy the scenery. Eventually a long line of boundary stones appears, part of a system extending many miles over the moor. They lead in a relentless straight line up over Piles Hill, but the track curves to follow the contours.

At the far side of the hill, the tramway swings away to the right **8** but you turn left towards the old Spurrell's Cross. Now you begin to head downhill towards the distant village of South Brent. As you descend the route becomes clearer. Just to the right of the nearer patch of woodland, the walls converge in a 'V', a drift which leads animals down to a gate at the apex. The walk goes the same way to join a green lane, an attractive footpath that leads off the moor to Owley. There is a final steep dip between high stone walls that brings you to the road where you turn left **9**.

Continue downhill past the cottages to cross a little brook almost lost among the trees, after which there is the inevitable steep climb back out of the valley. At the road junction **10** turn left, still climbing but nothing like so steeply. Now we are back with a familiar theme of the high-banked lane where every gateway provides a different view. At the end of quite a long climb, the road turns downhill again and there is a last reminder of the rougher moor in the form of a shapely gorse-covered hill. Then the road plunges more steeply down to a junction **11** where you turn left and immediately right. It ends at a bridge over the Avon by a small waterfall. Cross the bridge and turn right onto the riverside path that began the walk to return to South Brent.

# Winsford

This is one of those comfortable Exmoor villages, set down in a hollow and ringed by woodland. It boasts seven bridges, and even that is not enough, for cars on the road to Withypool still have to splash through a ford. It has a noble church with lofty interior and daunting Jacobean pulpit. At its heart is the inn with a roof that is a credit to the thatcher, with straw peacocks strutting along the ridge. It has been called the most beautiful village on Exmoor and few would disagree.

## WALK 1   Tarr Steps and the Barle Valley

13.5 miles (22 km)  See map on pages 78 and 79

This walk shows the many and varied aspects of Exmoor from open moorland to deep, wooded river valley, all linked by splendid undulating countryside.

From the village centre take the Tarr Steps road out past the Royal Oak. Once the houses are left behind, the route becomes quite steep, climbing up between high banks, and by the time the top is reached you get a clear view right across the valley to Dunkery Beacon. Crossing a cattle grid, where the road turns sharp left **1** continue straight on to the path onto the moor. Turn left on to either of the wide grassy tracks heading uphill – they rejoin quite soon. This is wonderful walking on close-cropped bouncy turf on a very open hillside with just a few shrubs poking above the bracken. Riders have created a complex of tracks up here, but the simple rule is to keep taking the most direct route to the top. Where the track divides **2**, turn right towards the rounded summit. Grass gives way to a rougher path which emerges above the great scooped-out hollow biting deep into the hill, The Punchbowl. Keep heading for the summit marked by a group of Bronze Age barrows and the stone pyramid of the trig point **A**. Now you can take a pause to enjoy the great panorama of Exmoor.

From the summit go down to the road and turn left. This is a quiet road with comfortable walking on the grassy margins and there is still open moorland to enjoy. Pass a footpath signpost on the

left, then by a second footpath sign **3,** just past a grassy clearing, turn right onto a clear, stony path heading down to the right across the moor. This becomes a grassy track that winds its way towards a clump of trees on the skyline. Where the path divides take the grassy track to the left, threading through the heather, bracken and bilberries. Once the trees are reached, they can be seen to be a tall beech hedge, which is followed downhill to a gate leading off the moor into the fields of the lower slopes. Carry on across the next two fields with the hedge on your right then continue on along a lane. Turn right on the surfaced track to reach Higher Knaplock Farm **4.** Turn right in front of the farm to farm buildings, where the track turns left to head downhill on the bridleway to Tarr Steps.

The track heads down towards the wooded valley spread out in front of you. Soon the way becomes much rougher and the clatter of stones as you descend causes much fluttering in the hedgerows. A stream is joined as the path enters the wood and there is a more gradual descent down to the banks of the Barle **5.** Turn left onto the path beside this beautiful river that glistens in the patches of sunlight filtering through the trees, as it rushes round a bend. The path follows the line of the river with, at one point, a high level bridleway and a low level footpath, the latter formed as a causeway of boulders. Either route can be taken, for they soon reunite by, what looks like, an alarming suspension bridge, but is only a device for stopping fallen trees. Beyond this, a short walk across grassland brings you to the most famous of clapper bridges, Tarr Steps **B**. It is of uncertain age and like grandad's old hammer, which has had two new heads and three new handles, it is hard to say what if anything has survived several rebuildings. Like all clapper bridges it consists of slabs laid on piles of stones acting as piers, but here extra slabs have been laid at an angle to the piers to act as crude cutwaters.

Cross the bridge and immediately turn off the road to the path to Hawkridge on the right which climbs very steeply past the hotel. It swings round past a wall, covered with moss-like organic flock wallpaper and then swings left again for a gentler climb to the brow of the hill, where there is a splendid old fashioned meadow, with a rich mixture of grasses, clover and flowers. Add to this the view out across the valley and back across to Winsford Hill and this is as good a stretch of country for walking as one could wish for. At the farm **6** where the way divides, keep straight on towards the farm buildings and join the farm approach road

The most famous of all the clapper bridges of south west England, Tarr Steps; of uncertain age, but probably medieval.

heading down towards the woods. The track now does a U-turn to cross a stream and head up through the woods on the opposite side of the valley. On reaching the road go straight across to continue on the Hawkridge path, and take a line parallel to the hedge and conifers on the left. Continue across the next field along the boundary between the bracken-covered slope and the grassland until a more obvious path is reached alongside the conifer plantation. Beyond a stile the path swings away from the woods to an obvious gap in the hedge and now you look down to the Barle valley again with its rich, green woodland setting. Go through the right-hand of two gates, waymarked in yellow, and head across the field to the houses.

At the road **7** turn left then right to Hawkridge church. This simple little building, restored in the nineteenth century, still has a few original Norman features, including the main door with its rather crudely carved columns and typical dogtooth decoration. Once past the church, where the road turns left, carry straight on down a track enclosed by beech hedges. After that the route continues to the right of the hedge and heads along the top of a ridge with woodland to either side. The very clear stony track now begins to head straight down to join the woodland dominated by sessile oak and beech. There is a gentle slope down to the river which promptly turns away again on a long meander and the path continues downhill, this time meeting a broad tributary, Dane's Brook. Cross Castle Bridge **C** named after two Iron Age hill forts, one on the hill to the north, its outline lost among the trees, and the other on the hill to the east.

Now we are back with a walk along the Barle, which has broadened considerably since we last met it at Tarr Steps. The wide path generally stays close to the water's edge, but where the hillside steepens it is forced to a higher level which provides a different perspective on the river scene. The river itself swings and twists, generally fast, clear and shallow, but occasionally being forced to dash more furiously through narrows. At the curiously named house, New Invention, the path joins a wider track, the woods disappear from the opposite bank and then, after passing a line of crags straggling down the hillside, the riverside walk ends at Marsh Bridge **8**.

Cross over the bridge, turn right and then left up the hill and take the rough path heading up through the woods to Court Down. This is an old lane, as is obvious from the size of the trees growing up from the banks on either side. It is a good, hard slog to the top and a track junction – a climb of over 400 ft (124m). At the junction **9** turn left onto the level track, then just past the gate, turn right to continue the climb to the top of Court Down. This is much easier walking with views right across to Dunkery Beacon. At the top of the field carry straight on through the gate

in front of you along the signposted bridleway, but it is worth a mini-detour into the field on the right to the trig point **D**. It does seem a shame after the effort involved in the climb not to go to the actual summit to enjoy the full panorama.

There is a lovely walk down with wide views over farmland, rounded hills and farms sheltering down in the hollows. The path heads straight down towards the cottage with a splendid multi-tiered chimney. Do not take the obvious track heading down to the right, but continue in the same direction across the field. At the next field turn right to a gate in the gap in the hedge. All the time the high viewpoint gives you a chance to enjoy a scene where everything seems to cohere – even the distant farmhouses seem to have grown out of the land. It is pure delight. Beyond double gates, the way continues to the left of the hedge, heading for a farm on the far side of a little, wooded valley. The path now drops down to the wood **10** and you turn left to follow the edge down to a gate which gives access. Take the path to the right which zigzags across the stream and up the bank on the far side to emerge by the farm. Go through the yard and turn left onto the farm road. This road-way turns sharp left to reach more barns **11** where you turn right onto the bridleway running between high banks. This comes out at double gates to an open path with a fence to the left, which is fol-lowed round to the left to a little conifer plantation. Carry on around the edge to reach the road **12** where you turn right.

This quiet lane leads up past Leigh Farm with a noisy, but largely invisible stream alongside. At the top of the hill where the view opens out **13** turn left on the broad bridleway for Winsford. Almost immediately, turn right through the gate to cut across the field at an angle from the road, heading for the right hand side of the line of trees on the skyline. Go to the right of a small disused quarry for the gate into the wood. The broad forest track is soon left for a decidedly interesting path diving down through the pines. Broadleaved trees now appear, making for a very pleasant descent that briefly rejoins the track and then takes the path again to the foot of the hill. Follow the edge of the wood round to the right for a short way until you reach a footbridge over a stream on the left **14**. Cross over a stile on the left, then turn right up the lane. This is a well used and churned bridleway, but fortunately walkers can take a drier path along the top of the bank. At the top of the climb, you look down on Winsford and a natural rock stair-case descends to the road **15**. Turn right to return to the start.

## WALK 2

### Exford and Dunkery Beacon

12 miles (19.5 km)  See map on pages 86 and 87

A lovely river valley provides the overture to the main theme, the climb to the highest point on Exmoor.

From the village centre, cross the footbridge beside the ford and follow the road up the hill past the church. As the hill levels out and the houses come to an end **1** turn right through a gate onto the footpath to Exford, which heads downhill under a canopy of beech. Where the track soon divides, carry on downhill to the right heading for the valley floor. The grassy track runs across a bracken-covered hillside to a gradually narrowing valley. Passing through a gate into woodland the path now joins the bank of the River Exe with steep slopes rising to either side. The meanderings of the river are closely followed, and the scene changes all the time, sometimes closed right in, sometimes opening out as the path rises and falls. Where tracks cross, stay by the riverside, now on a bridleway with a tempting view up ahead of the valley and its surrounding hills. For a time the river is a little less ebullient, and there is comfortable walking on a good, flat track but there is no lack of variety. The path slides in and out of patches of woodland, while the river itself occasionally abandons its calm progress for a sudden fall over rocks. Meanwhile the scenery is becoming increasingly dramatic with hills rising up ahead, so that it is almost impossible to see where the river might fit in. There is a brief opening out to the bracken-covered hill on the left before going into a lane between high banks. It was presumably once planted as a beech hedge, but the trees left to their own devices have grown and grown and now cling with claw-like roots to a very precarious perch. The river here is at its busiest, racing round boulders in a flurry of spray.

The track swings round to cross the river, and once across leave the bridleway for the permissive path to Exford **2**. The walk over the fields makes a pleasant change, and there is a fine old farm, typical of the area with its massive, square external chimney. Up ahead, the hills rise steeply and through them the river threads a narrow way. Go through a gap in the tall hedge to rejoin the river bank and leave the path by a gate next to a ford. Turn right up the hill to rejoin the bridleway and now having had a quiet riverside walk it is time to take an airier path along the

The path winding its way above the infant River Exe, which is a constant companion on the walk from Winsford to Exford.

flank of the hill. This gives you a chance to enjoy the scenery at its most dramatic as you look down on the river, almost lost from sight in its wooded gorge. Then the valley broadens out and the path once again descends to the valley floor. The river has wandered away to the left but the path is clear and the route indicated by blue marker posts. Eventually it emerges in a lane that leads down to the farm and the farm approach road.

Go past the traditional farmhouse to continue on the track, but immediately beyond the farmyard **3,** turn left over a stile to a footpath. At first it runs along the top of the field to keep clear of the marshy ground, but soon a line of yellow-topped posts indicate the route back to the river via a somewhat boggy path. It is with a certain relief that one reaches a stile leading to firmer ground near the river bank. Whether you can see fish in the clear water or not, they must be there for this stretch is well patrolled by heron. The route now keeps its distance from the water and once the open field is crossed a more obvious path is reached running beside fence and hedge. The path soon begins to climb again and once across a stile and into a large field you turn away from the river to follow the fence on the left uphill to the far corner of the field. Having climbed up it is now time to go down again on the track leading to the farm. Now the river is joined for the last time and a short stroll leads into the village of Exford **A**.

Follow the road into the centre of the village and the Crown Hotel which is a popular centre for the local stag hunt. It is a fine old inn but whether you enjoy a visit or not will depend on how you feel about having a pint under the glassy stare of several dead animals. From the hotel go up the road past the shop and post office. At the end of the playing fields **4** turn right up Combe Lane. The houses are soon left behind as the lane climbs steeply between ferny banks. Ignore the various footpaths leading away to either side and keep straight on along the bridleway which eventually becomes a rough track. This is a long, steady climb with not much in the way of views except at breaks in the confining high banks. The lane gradually sinks down into the land and branches meet overhead to form a cool, green tunnel. Where it opens out there is a wide vista to the left, but the hedge on the right keeps the rest hidden, though, of course, the higher you climb the more chances there are to look back to the neat pattern of tiny square fields below the darker moor. Reaching two gates, take the one on the right to continue on the opposite side of the hedge to find a brand new view, this time over to Dunkery Beacon with what, from here, looks like a little pimple of a cairn on the summit.

Reaching a track junction **5** turn left towards the road, where you cross and turn right for the path running alongside the road through typical moorland cover of coarse grass, heather and bilberry. There is a feeling of immense space and loneliness, with an almost featureless expanse of moor broken by patches of cotton grass over boggy ground and little to disturb the peace except the eerie cry of the curlew. At the road junction **6** turn right onto the bridleway beside the hedge at the edge of the moor. When eventually the hedge turns away down the hill, the majesty of the scene is finally unfolded. Looking down over the farmland it is a pleasure to see just how many hedgerows have survived in this region, crawling like thick furry caterpillars across the valleys and over the hills. For a time there is no obvious end in view, just moor spreading to the horizon until the cairn at the top of the hill pops into view. All that is necessary now is to follow the clear path to the summit **B**.

From the cairn, built in 1935 to record the handing over of the land to the National Trust, you get what is almost certainly the best view, and certainly from the highest point, on the whole of Exmoor – across the sea to Wales, south to Dartmoor and east to the Quantocks. A small panorama table just below the cairn identifies all the points of interest. After the long haul up, there is now a short, sharp descent by the obvious path to the car park. Carry straight on across the cattle grid and along the road still going downhill. Where the road swings left **7** turn right onto the broad track that immediately turns left to continue heading south towards Luckwell Bridge. This is another typical green lane closed in by hedges, but in compensation for not being able to see to either side there is an excellent view of the hills up ahead. Cross straight over the road to continue on the track, very busy with bounding rabbits. As the way steepens it gets rougher and plates of sandstone break the surface. By the end it has become a miniature gorge.

At the road **8** turn right and immediately left by the phone box. Cross the stone bridge and head up past the houses, beyond which you turn left up wooden steps set into the bank to join a footpath **9**. The path heads on a diagonal away from the wall to the end of the line of trees up ahead. Carry on uphill with the

The view looking out from Luckwell bridge to the distant hill of Dunkery Beacon, the highest point on Exmoor.

fence on the right and it is worth pausing to look back to the Beacon. Reaching a stile at the top of the hill, cut across the field to the far right corner for a gate and the path to the road. This brings you out by a T-junction and you keep going in the same direction past Oldrey Farm. The road climbs at first then levels out and begins to swing right **10** and here you carry on through the gate on the bridleway to Upcott Cross.

At first there is a view down to the deep cleft of the valley but then the banks close in. The path climbs steadily to cross the hill where everything opens out again, before the descent between banks highly coloured with foxglove and campion. Continue down past the farm entrance to the road **11** and turn right. If the banks of the lane were colourful, then those alongside this quiet road are doubly so with bryony, vetch and dog rose adding to the display. At the foot of the hill you reach the houses on the out-skirts of Winsford and turn left to cross Vicarage Bridge **12** to return to the centre.

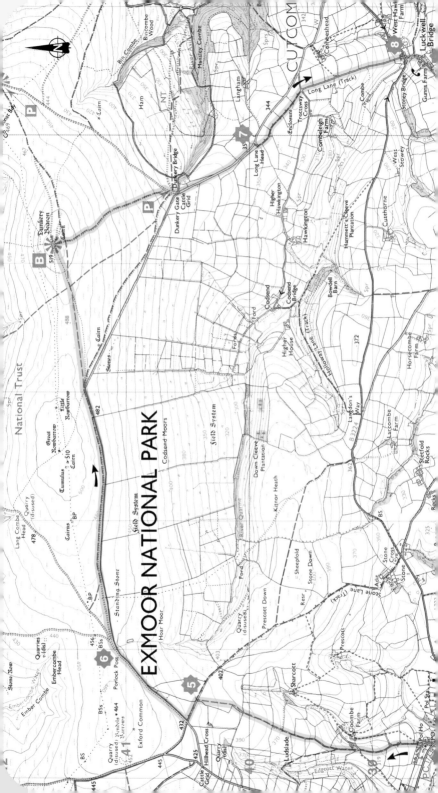

# Lynmouth

This beautiful little port has not had a happy history. The first harbour was detroyed by the sea in 1607 and even greater devastation was caused when the river flooded in 1952. Among the casualties was the 'Rhenish Tower' built to carry a light and act as a reservoir for sea bathing in 1860, but it like the rest of the town was rebuilt. Today, the town and the coastline on either side are famous beauty spots, as are the two river valleys, the East and West Lyn that converge here.

## WALK 1 — The Foreland and East Lyn Valley

12.5 miles (20 km)  See map on pages 92 and 93

The walk begins with a climb to the top of the high cliffs, heads inland to the famous 'Doone Valley' and enjoys a spectacular finale with the return down the dramatically beautiful East Lyn valley.

Leave the main street by the footbridge **1** across the river and continue along the sea front past the putting green. At the end of the stone wall turn right then immediately left onto the coast path heading up through the woods. At the start there is a grand array of beech trees, then a long steady climb up towards the road and, for walkers, the rather superfluous sign advising you to keep in lowest gear. A zigzag route comes out on a path which for a little way runs right beside the road. Turn left opposite the entrance to the Beacon Hotel to follow the path above the hawthorn-dotted slope that drops almost sheer to the sea. Now this is coastal walking at its best, on a grassy path heading off above a sweep of cliffs towards the massive headland of Foreland Point. Coming back almost to the road again, a short flight of steps leads up to an old gun emplacement and from there the way ahead can be seen as an insignificant grass ledge cut into the steep slopes that tumble away to the final drop to the sea, where the surf breaks with a pebbly crunch on shingle beaches. The Foreland seems to have its very own miniature weather system, for even on the clearest, bluest days it will often have a little white cap of cloud. You will know that the long climb has ended when you can look inland down to the valley.

The path leads towards Countisbury Church, but just before reaching it **2** turn to follow the stone wall on the right, then left to keep on the coastal path. This section is definitely not for vertigo sufferers, for it occupies a narrow ledge above a very steep drop – though if you did slip the worst that would happen would be a prickly entanglement with the gorse. This section ends above a deep, rocky cleft where sea pinks flourish. From here a broad swathe of a track leads to the top of the headland and a track crossing **3**. Turn right to cross over the neck of The Foreland, still following the South West Coast Path. At the far side there is a steep descent to the combe and the lighthouse approach road. Turn right onto the road **4** and, after a climb up to a point where the road doubles back through a hairpin bend, continue straight on along the track. The next part of the coastal walk is very different with woodland covering much of the slope above the cliffs. Cross a stile and climb wooden steps to reach a grassy path heading through scrub woodland, with patches of scree on the hillside and heather lining the path. Soon the path enters more established

Looking back along the coastal path towards Lynton and the wooded hillside above Lynmouth Bay.

woodland with just occasional glimpses of the sea through the trees. It crosses the head of a ravine-like combe with an almost tropical luxuriance of ferns clinging to the sides, soon followed by a second where a small stream trips down over the rocks. One more deep combe, then a gate leads out of the wood to a cliff path where masses of rhododendron bushes have established themselves. At the time of writing, a landslip has caused a path diversion with a steep climb up to the top of the cliffs and down again.

The route continues as a splendid coast path with great views of heather slopes and woodland high above the sea. At the next patch of wood the path turns inland round the edge of the wood and follows it round to the stream in the combe **5**. Here you continue inland up the side of the stream on the path signposted to White Gate. It climbs to the top of the gully where it levels out, but this is only a brief respite. It turns left round the shoulder of the hill for a vicious little climb through gorse and hawthorn to head up towards a band of conifers. A stile leads into the margin of the wood which is followed to the far side **6** where you turn left to make your way round the summit of Old Burrow Hill. At the centre of this area of grassland are the low earthworks of a Roman fort **A**. It is certainly very relaxing walking across the grass after the scramble up to this point for we are now over 1000 ft (305m) above the starting point on the shore. Beyond the fort a stile leads on to a broad track which turns right towards the road.

On reaching the road **7** cross over and turn right to the car park and then left onto the track through gorse and heather to County Gate **B**. There is a National Park Visitor Centre here and a picnic area, which gives a view down to the moor and a foretaste of the next part of the walk. Carry on back towards the road, then just before reaching it turn right through the gate onto the bridleway to Malmsmead. This is excellent walking on a grassy track that soon begins to lead down towards the valley on the right below the wooded hillside. At the foot of the hill, cross the river on the footbridge and go through the farmyard to the road **8** where you turn right, shortly followed by a left turn into the 'Doone Valley' past Cloud Farm. The 'Doone Country' tag owes a great deal to the nineteenth century romantic novel but not everything, for there really were fierce robber bands in this area in the seventeenth century. But it is the romance that is remembered, and across the water is Lorna Doone Farm, the original on which the Rudd family farm was based **C**. Meanwhile the surfaced path follows the

A narrow path above the cliffs provides a dramatic view of the headland at Foreland Point.

river down through the woodland to Cloud Farm, where you turn right to cross the footbridge **9** to continue on the opposite side of the little river with its bounding rapids. Continue upstream on an altogether rougher path through very much wilder scenery of heather, gorse and rock outcrops. The valley closes in and this picturesque spot was selected for the R. D. Blackmore memorial stone **D**. The walk now comes into oak woodland soon joined by conifers on the opposite bank. At a large clearing **10** turn right on the track up the valley, between two rounded hills.

At first the path follows the line of the stream down this wide valley surrounded by heather moorland, but soon it begins to turn right up the shoulder of the hill. This is very much lonely Exmoor, a landscape of distant horizons. At the gate, take the path to the left heading across typically peaty heather moorland. Where tracks cross carry straight on along the bridleway to Brendon. This runs down from the moor towards the fields, and continues as an obvious track that meets the road at a T-junction **11**. Turn left along the road, which bends steeply down towards the little wooded valley you can see snaking away on the right. After another steep drop, the road bends sharply to the right and after about 30 paces, turn right onto the path through the woods signposted to Rockford **12**. There is a wild little stream rushing down the hillside and the path takes an equally precipitous route beside it. At the foot is an old mill with its waterwheel still in place.

At the road **13** turn left and now you have the rushing East Lyn alongside, which is to be a companion for the rest of the walk. At the foot of the hill by the houses of Rockford **14**, turn right to cross the river on the footbridge then left onto the riverside walk. Here the river is at its most dramatic – channelled down by rocks, it roars down falls and hurtles through gullies. There are a number of paths through the woods but the Fisherman's Path is particularly attractive, closely following the twists and turns of the river. Inevitably in such a confined valley the path has to fit in where it can, so that although the river heads at high speed to the sea, the walker seems to spend as much time going uphill as down.

At Watersmeet **E** where the river is swollen by a tributary, the route continues past the old stone bridge, still keeping to the same bank of the river. The water is now a good deal calmer and the path takes a high level route above the river for much of the way. The final approach to Lynmouth passes under sandstone cliffs, the river is rejoined and a paved path leads back to the start.

## WALK 2   Parracombe and Woody Bay

12.5 miles (20 km)  See map on pages 100 and 101

There is a gentle beginning after reaching Lynton with a walk through farmland, but the scenery becomes ever more dramatic as a deep river valley leads back to the coast. The final section offers coastal walking of the highest quality.

There is more than one way to start this walk. One could move it to Lynton, but those who want to walk the whole route from Lynmouth should take the tarmac path that winds up the hill from Lynmouth Street **1**. At the top of the path, turn left to the church then right down the main road to the rather exotic town hall, which seems to have crept over from the Black Forest. The third and perhaps most interesting option – and it is not really cheating since you can walk back down the cliff path at the end – is to take the cliff railway. Opened in 1890, it uses a water balance system. The two cars run on twin tracks and have water tanks built in. When the one at the top is filled, the extra weight takes it down the hill, pulling its partner up. It is great fun. Whichever option is taken the description now continues from the town hall **2**.

Take the road opposite the town hall, Cross Street and then turn right at the T-junction. Where the main road turns through a hairpin bend carry straight on up the minor road marked as a dead end **3**. This road has now been declared unsuitable for motor vehicles so that it has become, in effect, a bridleway. There is a steep climb to begin with, which gradually eases but the road continues to rise steadily for about a kilometre. As so often, there are banks and hedges beside the road, with gaps that provide snapshot views of the surrounding country – first of the spectacular Valley of Rocks, then of the surrounding farmland with its tidy pattern of fields spreading out over all the surrounding hills. These are typical Enclosure Act fields planned on a map and bearing no relation to the contours of the land.

Reaching the top of the hill, the view begins to open out and there is a gradual descent to the hill that rises straight ahead. On reaching the road **4** carry straight on past the caravan park, and topping a little rise, the busy traffic on the A39 comes into sight. At the T-junction **5** turn right onto a very quiet country lane that passes the end of a combe then begins to climb round the shoulder of the hill. What appears at first as an odd little tower turns out to be a tall chimney stack – all that remains of an old cottage, a monument to the durability of those external stacks that are such a feature of traditional Exmoor houses. The road continues through farmland. It dips to cross a stream with sheep pens beside then climbs out of the hollow again. Where it levels out **6** turn left over the stile at the end of the stone wall.

Cross over the field of rough grass and gorse, keeping parallel to the fence and wall on the left and cross the stile for a brief revisit to the road. Turn left and after about 300 ft (100 m) where the road begins to turn left, turn right through a gate to join the footpath. At the end of the first field on the left turn left through the gate onto the bridleway leading towards the A39, which runs across the face of the hill up ahead. But for now, the path goes down beside the fence to the stream which is crossed to a gate leading to an obvious path. Once through the next gate the track swings round to the right. Eventually you reach a large open field with splendid views down to the hamlet of Killington which manages to combine a picturesque position at the head of a combe with the comfort of a sheltering hollow. Take a line across the field passing the end of an isolated wall jutting out into the middle, after which a definite landmark appears and you head for the road sign on the A39.

At the road **7** turn right and stay with the main road to the junction where you turn right up the minor road to Hunter's Inn with a view out across to the headland rising high above the sea. At the next junction, turn left again and then almost immediately left through a gate onto the footpath to Parracombe Lane **8**. Cross the field keeping to the hedge and continue in the same direction via gates and stiles enjoying fine views of the distant landscape where the chequered farmland gives way to the darker, open spaces of the high moor, while closer at hand the houses of Parracombe come into view. Cross a stile **9** to join the road and turn right to go steeply downhill into the village.

At the crossroads **10** turn right on the dead end road which leads to the attractive hamlet of Bodley and turn right up the bridleway **11**. It might seem perverse not to take the more direct path, but it is well worth the extra effort, for once you have completed the little climb you turn left onto the bridleway to West Hill **12** for a splendid high level route. There is time to take in all the surrounding countryside as you keep to this level across two fields before the path turns slightly downhill to a track crossing **13**. Turn right onto the footpath with a low bank to the left. This

The path sweeps round the hillside above the deep, wooded cleft of the Heddon Valley.

is splendid walking, heading down towards the wooded valley that will provide the route back to the coast. As the fields end, the track becomes rougher, the sound of water grows louder and you arrive at the infant River Heddon where you turn right.

This does not yet have a very river-like quality. It is more of a mountain stream, but powerful enough to turn the wheels of the old Burnsley Mill **A** now the centre of a little housing development. The valley becomes increasingly attractive the further down you go. Narrow, wooded and steep, the accompanying river leaps down in torrent after torrent. A footbridge **14** gives you a chance to cross the stream for a short meander through oak and beech before returning on a second bridge. On reaching Mill Farm continue on the wide track and some intriguing names appear on the way for there is a house called Tucking Mill and a little settlement called Milltown. This was, unlikely as it may seem in such a wild setting, a minor centre of the woollen industry. Cloth was brought here from the weavers to be pounded by water-powered hammers in a fulling mill which shrank the cloth and created a much closer weave. This section of the walk ends at the popular Hunter's Inn **B**.

Leave the road for the track up the wooded hill on the right, a good stiff climb above a green cleft packed with trees. When the long climb eventually emerges above the trees the whole drama of the scene becomes apparent for the first time. Across the narrow valley a hill rises almost sheer, scattered with gorse and scree and there is a glimpse of the little bay of Heddon's Mouth, a favourite haunt of smugglers centuries ago. The path makes a great turn round the end of a combe and there is a last chance to enjoy the magnificent view down the valley, but more grandeur lies up ahead. Now the track heads on to reach rocky outcrops over 600 ft (193m) above the sea, and the route ahead can be seen running enticingly above the high cliffs.

The path now runs at a high level, just above the South West Coast Path and it is a truly spectacular length of coastline. Heather slopes fall steeply down from the path and a series of jagged rocks jut out from the base of the cliffs. the path passes the old Roman fortlet of Martinhoe **C** established around AD 60. Protected by ramparts and ditches, there were wooden barracks for a centuria of 80 men who kept watch over the Channel. Passing yet another great scoop out of the coast, another fine view opens out to a series of rocky headlands. Then a gate leads into woodland and the views are lost, reduced to tantalising glimpses of pebbly bays far below. But wherever a gap appears in the trees there, it seems, someone has placed a bench so that the view can be admired in comfort and one can sit and wonder just how trees manage to cling to such precipitous slopes.

The trees come to an end and the track continues as a road carrying on downhill, which leads directly into the Lynton toll road. This is a famously scenic route, and it soon shows off its attractions. It sweeps round above a deep gully, where a stream makes its long, last drop to the sea. Rocks loom out through the trees as the road makes its way above Woody Bay, and it is no problem hunting for the origin of the name. At the beautifully situated Woody Bay Hotel, the route joins the long distance footpath. Again there are snatched glimpses of tall cliffs and rocks thrust far out into the sea. The woods finally end at Lee Bay.

The road now heads inland towards a very grand house, Lee Abbey. It was originally a manor house, but was totally rebuilt in the fashionable Gothic style in 1845. It was bought by the Anglican Church in 1945 and established as a residential centre – and some incongruous concrete extensions were added. Reaching the top of the hill beyond the abbey one is greeted by the fantastical rock formations and pinnacles that do look sufficiently like turrets and battlements to justify the name Castle Rock. Where the road bends round to the right **15** continue on the footpath which makes a grand finale to the coastal path, a narrow, cliff-hugging walkway above sheer cliffs and rocks where the local wild goats hop around with supreme nonchalance. Turning the corner back into Lynmouth Bay, extravagant turreted houses come into view, then the path crosses the line of the cliff railway to reach the top of the path **2** for the return to Lynmouth.

The Valley of Rocks ends at this spectacular formation that provides a visual climax to the walk back to Lynmouth.

The long, stiff climb up from Porlock to the top of Bossingon Hill is rewarded by this magnificent view.

# Porlock

A town known for its poetical associations. Coleridge was famously interrupted by 'the man from Porlock' after he had started writing *Kubla Khan* – and was never able to finish it. Southey very sensibly spent a good deal of time in The Old Ship Inn penning his verses. It is a place of great charm. Its thirteenth-century church boasts a splendid canopied tomb and just up the road fifteenth-century Doverhay Court houses a small museum. Not least of Porlocks attractions is its position, as good a centre for coastal walks as it is for exploring the open spaces of the moor.

## WALK 1 — Selworthy Beacon and Horner

11 miles (18 km)  See map on pages 106 and 107

Starting with a climb to Selworthy Beacon high above the sea, the walk makes its way inland for a walk across the open moor, before returning down a deep, wooded valley.

From the main street, turn up Sparkhayes Lane heading towards the sea and passing a large camp site on the left. Just before the tarmac ends **1** turn right up steps marked Coast Path Bossington and carry on up the road to the junction where you turn left onto a path running between high hedges with the sea coming into view and the remains of old lime kilns on the beach. Follow the path round to the right, go through a kissing gate and continue along the edge of the field. Although the path crosses the hedge twice it continues heading towards the headland of Hurlstone Point and eventually joins a lane leading to the houses at Bossington. At this attractive village of stone and thatch, the walk joins the South West Coast Path with its acorn waymarks.

At the road **2** turn right and follow it round to the left, then turn by the phone box into the car park  at the far side of which a footbridge leads on to a bridleway. Turn left, initially following the stream, but soon turning away to begin a gentle climb up the wooded slope. As the trees clear the height and steepness of the hill becomes dauntingly clear and to make matters worse, having just made a start up the hill, the path now dips down again to beach level. Now the broad track gives way to a narrower path that begins to climb in earnest, then turns inland **3** for a much steeper climb up Hurlstone Combe, with a scree-covered slope to the side. This is a really stiff climb that eventually reaches a seat at the top **A** which serves a double purpose: it gives you a chance to get your breath back and to admire the view over Porlock Bay and across the Channel to the Welsh coast. After that the path carries straight on following the coastal route to Minehead through gorse bushes which provide convenient perches for stonechats, cheerful little birds that seem remarkably unconcerned by passing walkers. The grassy track becomes stonier and leaves the gorse behind for coarse moorland grass. Coming over the shoulder of Bossington Hill a whole new vista begins to open out as the sea views are joined by a distant prospect of woodland and the hills of Exmoor. At the very top of the hill, the path is joined by another track coming up from the valley, after which the way divides **4**. Keep to the left, following the acorn markers. The scenery constantly changes, with rough grazing land coming in on the right. Where paths divide, keep to the left, still following the coast path as it makes its way through gorse and heather. Carry straight on across a farm approach road and the path continues on the edge of fields. The farm itself can be seen, snug in its shelter of trees with a deep combe below it heading steeply to the sea. Here where the path divides **5** turn right onto the path running between high banks of gorse and then turn left at the next track junction to join the road near a cattle grid. Continue in the same direction beside the road for about 500 ft (150 m) to a signpost for the bridleway via Wydon Farm **6**. Turn right to go down the hill.

The path goes through an area of pasture grazed by cattle and sheep with occasional patches of rich, red earth of arable land. Down to the left there is a glimpse of Minehead and the bay while over to the right is an attractive wooded combe. Now the birds of the coast give way to those of wood and moor with the local crows showing their obvious distaste for any buzzard getting near their territory. The path passes through the gap in the line of trees on the left, then carries on downhill to pass to the left of the farm buildings, and you take the path through the farmyard and on down to the road. Now one is in a familiar Somerset landscape of lanes running between bank and hedge with a distant prospect of softly rounded hills crowned by trees. Carry straight on at the road junction and follow the road round to the right to Hindon Farm, a delightful spot with ducks and geese to quack and hiss you on your way **7**.

Turn left on the path signed to Selworthy and go through a gate to climb the hill, with more views back to Minehead. Carry straight on along the road beside the wood, then as the road turns left at the edge of the plantation, turn right onto the bridleway to Selworthy Beacon. An avenue of oak leads up towards the farm, but before reaching that point, turn left **8** onto the grassy track down to the main road. Cross straight over onto the minor road to Tivington. Pass splendid old Tivington Farm, very traditional apart from an unusual timber framed porch. There is now a steady climb up to Troyte's Farm, where you continue up the lane marked as a dead end. This is a little green tunnel with a fresh herby smell, like walking through a salad. Carry straight on along the footpath for Huntscott. The surfaced road ends and gives way to a track that ends by the last of the houses. Turn left onto the path with the conifer plantation on the right and where the woodland ends follow the bottom end of the field round to the left. Go through a gap in the hedge and now the route lies across the field, but is far from obvious. The easiest route is to keep a little way from the boundary on the right until you reach a stream, then turn left along it until you reach a footbridge **9**. Once across there is a clear path to a gate at the far side of the wood. Turn right to find a stile and now the way is very clear with a long strip of woodland over to the right of the path, which proceeds by a series of stiles and a footbridge until it reaches the road at Huntscott **10**.

Turn left along the road into Huntscott, a place of exotic birds, where guinea fowl scatter under the aloof gaze of peacocks. Opposite Huntscott House stables, turn right up the hill along a sunken lane, completely arched over by trees. At the top of a steady climb, cross the stream and turn right onto the bridleway. Then, at the obvious gap in the trees **11**, turn left to head uphill once again to reach the path that can be clearly seen running across the face of the moor. On reaching this sandy path turn right for a pleasant moorland stroll. There is a splendid view, looking out over the village of Luccombe, standing at the head of the wooded valley that will provide the route back to Porlock. The immediate surroundings are typical of Exmoor, an uninterrupted spread of heather and bracken with just a few stunted trees that have struggled to raise their heads but have been forced to submit and bow their heads to the wind. Follow the path down to the road by the edge of the wood **12** and turn right. The road begins to head downhill through mature mixed woodland and as

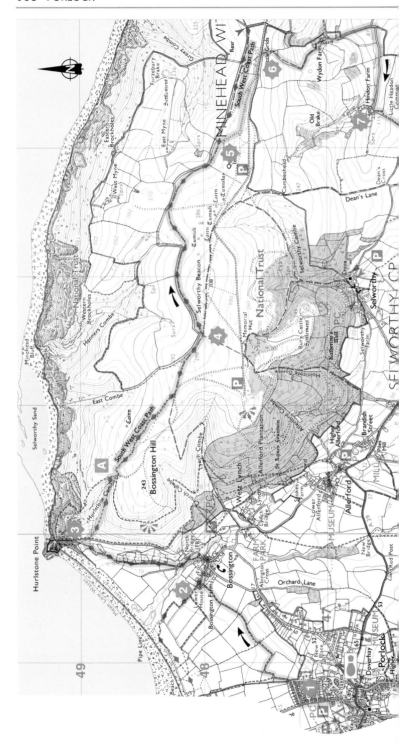

A high-arched packhorse bridge, with cobbled roadway and low parapets, crosses the hill stream at Horner.

it begins to steepen look out for a path on the left, signposted to Horner. This runs parallel to the road for a way then becomes a wide forest track with a boundary ditch and bank topped by beech. As the path gets lower down the hill, so the trees become ever more majestic with the beech as undisputed kings of this forest. The path ends at a gate which leads on to the road and a continuation of the descent into Horner. This hamlet enjoys a most beautiful setting with its high surrounding wall of trees.

Where the cottages come to an end, turn left over the bridge **B**. This is a typical old high-arched packhorse bridge with a cobbled surface. One might wonder what was being carried to and from this tiny settlement, but at one time Horner could boast a fulling mill for finishing cloth and a small iron furnace. Once across the bridge, follow the path down by the stream to the path to Luckbarrow. This now takes an attractive high level route above the stream and stays in the woods until it rejoins the road **13**. Turn left and at the road junction carry straight on down the hill. Now you can look ahead to Porlock Bay, before the road dips down through woodland bright with rhododendron for a final steep descent back into Porlock.

| WALK 2 | Culbone and Oare |
|---|---|

14 miles (22.5 km)  See map on pages 114, 115 and 116

The coastal path again starts the walk, but this time along the wooded hills above the sea. Inland there is a visit to Oare, forever associated with *Lorna Doone* and a return via moorland and a beautiful river valley.

Leave Porlock on the A39 heading towards Lynton. Continue left on the main road at the edge of the village, then turn right onto the toll road. Where the houses come to an end **1** turn right onto the coastal path by the acorn sign. Soon you get a good view out over the eerie flooded landscape of Porlock Bay, where the sea burst through the defences to form a salt marsh with skeletal trees poking forlornly above the water. Then the view is lost behind the sweet scented trees of a luxuriant garden. The rough path wanders through a mixed wood where the native birch, beech and oak alternate with denser patches of conifer – and there are occasional bird's eye views into more exotic gardens. The path climbs then drops again to a broad track leading to a driveway. Cross straight over and continue down to the road **2** where you turn left, then left again. At the next road junction, turn right towards Porlock Weir **A**.

The little port was created when the sea retreated from Porlock itself in the fifteenth century. It was improved in 1855 with the construction of quay, harbour and lock gates, but it is now home to pleasure craft and the occasional fishing boat. From the harbour, take the path behind the Anchor Hotel which leads away from the village and back up to the road. At the road, turn right and after a short distance one reaches the ornate archway of Worthy Lodge **3** where motorists pay a toll, but walkers pass free through the arch on the right for a path that clambers up into the woods. These woods have a sombre history, a place of banishment in medieval times, a prison colony, and in the sixteenth century a leper colony. After that they became cheerier, appreciated for their picturesque qualities, so that the walk includes an ornate castellated bridge and even a short tunnel. This was once an approach road to a grand house, now demolished, and the owner had the tunnel made so that approaching tradesmen would not sully his view. The path generally follows a long, steady climb, but in places zigzags up the steep slopes, with the occasional little rock seat providing a chance to pause and enjoy the sea view.

Passing craggy outcrops, the path drops down to the hamlet of Culbone **B** with another picturesque arched building. This is a beautiful spot where the stream hurries down over rock ledges past a tiny church, said to be the smallest complete church in the country, almost certainly founded in Saxon times and mentioned in Domesday Book. It has a simple, unassuming charm. From here the path continues towards Lynmouth, climbing then doubling back to leave the woods for a lane of flowered banks and hedges, and passing through a landscape of rolling hills and woods. A steep final climb brings you out at imposing Silcombe Farm from where the path continues signposted to Broomstreet Farm. Follow the tarmac path round past the farm, where there is a brief chance to look down on the sea again, before joining a farm track with a tall beech hedge protecting the fields from salty breezes. Where the tall hedge changes sides, the view returns. Eventually it all opens out to the distant headland of Foreland Point and gorse moors, before it all disappears again as the path curves away between high banks to emerge above a wooded combe. Cross a little stream, the first of many as the path switchbacks crossing the heads of combes where the hill streams busy themselves in the rush to the sea. Eventually

The tiny church founded over 1000 years ago at Culbone.

you reach a paved approach road which leads up to Broomstreet Farm. Turn right to continue on the Lynmouth path through lovely countryside of hills and knolls, grassy slopes and little combes sliding away to the sea. The path becomes less distinct after a while, no more than a dip in the ground beside a gorse topped wall. This section ends at a gate by a large open field where the way divides **4**. Here the coastal path turns back to the sea, but the walk goes straight on along the permissive path to Yenworthy Farm.

The route is quite indistinct, but a post in the field acts as a way-mark, beyond which a clearer path leads through the trees to a stile by a stream. Now the path leads forward and on to another field with a waymarker. Beyond that a gate brings you out by the remarkably handsome stone farmhouse. Turn left to follow the footpath along the edge of the field in front of the farm and then turn left onto the farm approach road. The road climbs up past a tangled wood to heather moorland and the main road. Cross straight over to the stile and the path leading down to Oare. It runs down to the right of Oare House in a wide loop. At the farmyard cross the stile on the right for the path above the farm then take the stile on the left and carry on down to the stile by the gate **5**.

Turn left at the road. The walk turns off at the bridge but a very short extra walk brings you to the church **C**. In the novel *Lorna Doone*, Lorna was shot here on her wedding day. There is nothing the least violent now about this little church with its box pews, and it does have one reminder of its fictional fame – a memorial to the author R. D. Blackmore beside the door. Return to the bridge **6**, cross over and turn right onto the riverside path. There is a short pleasant grassy walk beside the tumbling river, then after crossing a tributary stream turn left past an old wooden cottage and follow the stream round to reach a lovely little valley scooped out of the moor. Take the path up through the gorse to reach the rim of the valley which is then followed round to its head where you turn away to the right to join a wide grassy track 7. This heads straight across the middle of a great expanse of gorse-patched heather. Where a fence approaches the track on the right, the way becomes less distinct but heading to the right of the trees up ahead you will reach a gate and a precipitous descent into a beautiful deep valley.

At the foot of the hill, cross the footbridge and turn left to the road **8**. High hills, pine-topped knolls and a rushing river all add to the pleasures of the scene. Cross the river at Robber's Bridge and where the road turns right **9** continue straight on along the

Looking down from the hillside path above Robber's Bridge to the lovely Weir Water valley.

bridleway to Culbone Inn. Once through the gate, follow the path as it works its way round the shoulder of the hill, providing a constantly changing viewpoint, first of the Weir Water down in the valley and then of the combe. This is clearly an old road, with a hint of a cobbled surface, but now all is peace apart from the short sharp calls of grey wagtails, the eerie mew of the buzzard and the less melodic cries of pheasant in the woods. At the head of the valley, take the track round the back of the inn to the road. Cross straight over to the road opposite running through the conifers. As the road swings right and begins to head downhill **10** turn right onto the forest track heading steeply down through the trees. Porlock Bay can be seen up ahead and the way down grows ever steeper – with the slightly depressing sight of an equally steep hill that has to be climbed across the valley. At the foot of the hill, cross the stream and continue following it downstream to a track junction by Pitt Farm, where you turn right for the climb up to the road.

At the junction by the car park **11** turn left onto the main road and immediately right onto the track across the heather moorland. This brings you down to a minor road where you turn left **12** and look out on the right for the bridleway to Porlock. The grassy path heads down to a little gully with a stream in the bottom. The route veers away from the deepening valley to become a narrow path through the heather, gradually steepening as it heads down to enter the woods. This develops into a splendid walk through woodland dominated by sessile oak, and as the valley sinks ever deeper into the land so the path becomes ever rougher, running below steep slopes of scree. The stream is crossed and recrossed until you arrive at a meeting of ways offering alternative routes back to Porlock **13**. But this little valley is too lovely to desert, so continue straight on along the line of the stream towards Hawkcombe. The path waymarked by blue patches on the trees keeps close to the water, where dippers hop around on the rocks. As the valley descends and broadens, the vegetation becomes lusher, the trees taller and soon houses come into view. Pass a rather grand hunting lodge, followed by a charming and aptly named cottage, Peep-out.

There is a substantial stepped weir across the stream, a clear indication that the water has been used for power. In fact the old Hawkcombe Mill **D** was adapted in 1909 for use as a hydro-electric station. The track runs past the water mill, its overshot wheel still in place, and gradually improves into a proper road that ends beside Porlock Church.

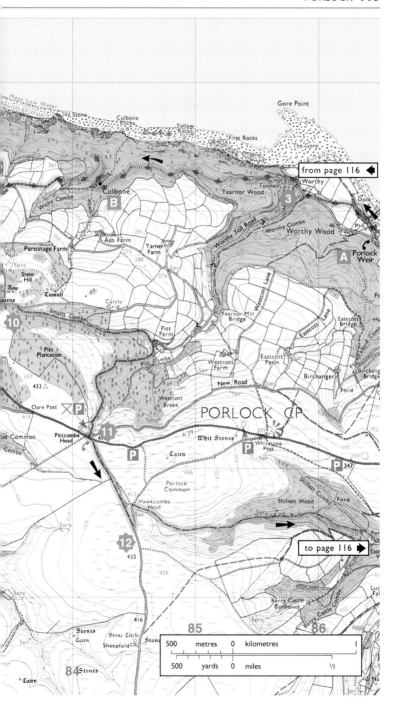

from page 116 ◀

to page 116 ▶

Gore Point

The Gore

Mean Low Water

Ivy Stone

Culbone Rocks

Yellow Rocks

First Rocks

Worthy

Dock

PH

Culbone

Yearnor Wood

Tunnels Toll

Worthy Combe

Worthy Wood

**A** Porlock Weir

Withy Combe

Parsonage Farm

Ash Farm

Yarner Farm

Worthy Toll Road

Stent Hill

Spr

Row

Cairns

Tumuli

Cattle Grid

Smalls Combe

Pitt Farm

Yearnor Mill Bridge

Westcott Lane

Eastcott Lane

Eastcott Bridge

Birchanger Bridge

**10**

Pitt Plantation

433

Pitt Combe

Westcott Farm

Eastcott Farm

Birchanger

Ford

Oare Post

New Road

Westcott Brake

**PORLOCK** CP

**11**

Pittcombe Head

Oare Common

Combe

Whit Stones

Whitstone Post

P 347

Cairn

Porlock Common

Shillett Combe

Ford

Hawkcombe Head

Shillett Wood

**12**

433

429

Berry Castle Earthwork

Berry Castle Combe

Stones Cairn

Stone Circle

Sheepfold

**84** Stones

Cairn

**85**

**86**

| 500 | metres | 0 | kilometres | | 1 |
|-----|--------|---|------------|---|---|
| 500 | yards  | 0 | miles      | | 1/2 |

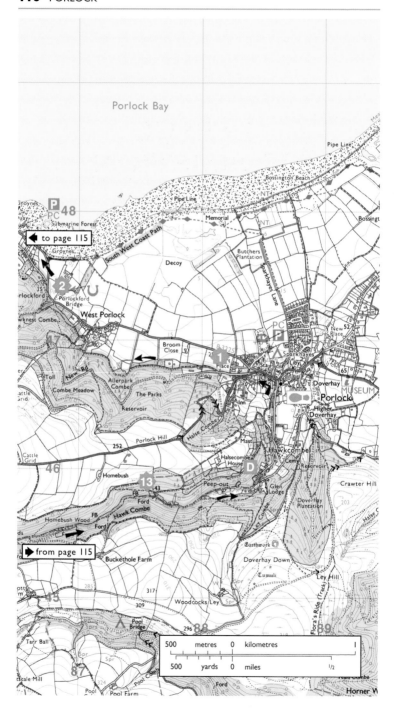

Porlock Bay

to page 115

from page 115

# USEFUL
# INFORMATION

# Accommodation on Dartmoor and Exmoor

The National Park authorities for both Dartmoor and Exmoor publish free information newspapers annually, *Dartmoor Visitor* and *Exmoor Visitor* and these give useful advice on all aspects of the two parks, including accommodation. Tourist information centres for the parks can also be contacted or one of the many bed and breakfast guides can be consulted. The YHA has a number of hostels in the area and can be contacted at Trevelyan House, 8 St Stephen's Hill, St Albans, Herts AL1 2DY (tel: 01727 855215).

### *Youth Hostels*
**Dartmoor**
Bellever, Postbridge, Yelverton PL20 6TU (tel: 01822 880227)
 GR 191/ 654773
Steps Bridge, Nr Dunsford, Exeter EX6 7EQ
 (tel: 01647 252435) GR 191/ 802882
Dartington, Lownard, Dartington, Totnes TQ9 6JJ
 (tel: 01803 862303) GR 202/ 782622
**Exmoor**
Exford, Exe Mead, Exford, Minehead TA24 7PU
 (tel: 10643 831288) GR 181/ 853383
Lynton, Lynbridge, Lynton EX35 6AZ (tel: 01598 753237)
 GR 180/ 720487
Minehead, Alcombe Combe, Minehead TA24 6EW
 (tel: 01643 703016) GR 181/ 973442

# Tourist Information Centres
**Dartmoor**
Ivybridge, Leonards Road, Ivybridge PL21 0SL
 (tel: 01752 897035)
Okehampton, 3 West Street, Okehampton EX20 1HQ
 (tel: 01837 53020)

Tavistock, Town Hall, Bedford Square, Tavistock PL19 0AE
(tel: 01822 612938)
**Exmoor**
Lynton & Lynmouth, Town Hall, Lee Road, Lynton EX35 6BT
(tel: 01598 752225)
Minehead, 17 Friday St, Minehead TA24 5UB
(tel: 01643 702624)

# DARTMOOR NATIONAL PARK

Headquarters: Dartmoor National Park, Parke, Haytor Rd, Bovey
Tracey TQ13 9JQ (tel: 01626 832093)
High Moorland Visitor Centre, The Old Duchy Building,
Tavistock Rd, Princetown PL20 6QF (tel: 01822 890414)
Information centres at Haytor (tel: 01364 661520), Newbridge
(tel: 01364 631303) and Postbridge (tel: 01822 880272)

# DARTMOOR FIRING RANGES

Details of firing times can be obtained from the telephone
answering service – 0800 4584868

# EXMOOR NATIONAL PARK

Headquarters: Exmoor National Park, Exmoor House, Fore St,
Dulverton TA22 9HL (tel: 01398 323665)
Visitor Centres
Combe Martin, Seacot, Cross Street, Combe Martin
(tel: 01271 883319)
County Gate, A39 Countisbury (tel: 01598 741321)
Dulverton, Fore St, Dulverton (tel: 01398 323841)
Dunster, Dunster Steep, Dunster (tel: 01643 821835)
Lynmouth, The Esplanade, Lynmouth (tel: 01598 752509)

# LOCAL WEATHER REPORTS, METEROLOGICAL OFFICE WEATHERCALL

Somerset 0906 8500405; Devon & Cornwall 0906 8500404

# ORDNANCE SURVEY MAPS

**Dartmoor**
Outdoor Leisure Map 28 (1:25,000);
Landranger Maps 191, 201, 202 (1:50,000)

**Exmoor**
Outdoor Leisure Map 9 (1:25,000) ;
Landranger Maps 180, 181 (1:50,000)